# PRANG'S CIVIL WAR PICTURES

# THE NORTH'S CIVIL WAR SERIES

Paul A. Cimbala, Series Editor

# Prang's
## CIVIL WAR PICTURES
### THE COMPLETE BATTLE CHROMOS OF LOUIS PRANG

With the Full "Descriptive Texts"

Edited with an Introduction by Harold Holzer

Fordham University Press

New York

2001

Copyright © 2001 by Fordham University Press

The publication of this book was made possible through the support of Furthermore,
a program of the J. M. Kaplan Fund.

The North's Civil War, No. 16
ISSN 1089-8719

Library of Congress Cataloging-in-Publication Data
Prang, Louis, 1824–1909.
Prang's Civil War pictures : the complete battle chromos of Louis Prang with the full
"descriptive tests" / edited with an introduction by Harold Holzer.—1st ed.
p.  cm.—*The North's Civil War ; no. 16)
Includes bibliographical references and index.
ISBN 0-8232-2118-0 (hc)
1. United States—History—Civil War, 1861–1865—Campaigns—Pictorial works.
2. United States—History—Civil War, 1861–1865—Campaigns.  3. Chromolithography—
United States—History—19th century.  I. Holzer, Harold.  II. Title.  II. Series.

E470.P68 2001
973.7'3—dc21

2001023604

Printed in the United States of America
01  02  03  04  05   5  4  3  2  1
First Edition

# CONTENTS

Contents

# PROLOGUE

*B*etween 1886 and 1888, L. Prang & Company, the nation's most famous and successful publisher of decorative color prints for the family home, issued a series of eighteen chromolithographs of some of the best-known land and sea battles of the Civil War.

More than twenty-five years had passed since Americans had fought fellow Americans at Antietam or Gettysburg, but Prang's battlefield chromos, designed specifically for Union veterans and their descendants, touched a chord with the public. They helped to ignite a wave of nostalgia and patriotic recollection, forever fixing the great scenes and heroes of the "late war" in national memory.

The large, handsome chromos became instant best-sellers and remained a staple of the Prang Company's catalogues for a generation. The prints claimed honored places in American parlors until the turn of the century, when the taste for such decorations began to fade. Ever since, the chromos have remained familiar to Civil War aficionados through their frequent use as illustrations on dust jackets, in history books, and in magazines.

Yet, amazingly, they have never before been published as a complete portfolio in book form. And the comprehensive "Descriptive Texts" that accompanied the original chromos in the late 1880s—a promotional premium that offered insightful history in the bargain—have been all but lost to readers ever since they first appeared.

This book reunites the pictures and text for the first time. Prang's "War Pictures" help us vividly recall how Americans kept the story of their worst national nightmare alive—and, somehow, reassuring—into a new age.

# ACKNOWLEDGMENTS

$\mathcal{M}$any scholars and curators provided crucial help during the long effort to bring this book into print. It is a pleasure to take this opportunity to thank all of them.

Above all, I am grateful to Elliot Davis, now principal curator for American Art at the Museum of Fine Arts, Boston. Earlier in her career, as an American Art curator (and colleague) at The Metropolitan Museum of Art in New York, she gave me complete access to the museum's copy of Prang's *Descriptive Texts* and allowed me to copy and use them for this volume. This project could not have been undertaken without her enthusiastic cooperation, or the valuable help of the staff of the Metropolitan's Thomas J. Watson Library.

Bernard Reilly of the Chicago Historical Society has been a respected colleague and advisor since his days at the Library of Congress, and while still there he was kind enough to provide a reproduction of an important print that had been taken out of circulation to be digitalized. He also made available Chicago's copy of the bound Prang *Descriptive Texts*. I am most grateful as well to the current staff at the Library of Congress's Prints & Photographs Division, who gave me unlimited access to its vast Prang holdings. And Deborah

Evans of the Library's Prints & Photographs Division was, as always, helpful, prompt, and efficient in supplying both color and black-and-white illustrations. So was Cindy VanHorn at the Lincoln Museum in Fort Wayne, who provided the elusive reproduction of the one Prang war picture missing from the Library of Congress's archive.

Sinclair Hitchings and Jane Duggan at the Boston Public Library offered a valuable reading of the introductory text and most generously provided copies of Prang materials from that institution's pre-eminent collection. And Kenneth M. Newman of the legendary Old Print Shop in New York City graciously granted permission to copy one of the Prang prints from his catalogues. Peter Harrington of the Anne S. K. Brown Military Collection of the John Hay Library at Brown University in Providence helped me find the original Thure de Thulstrup watercolor of *Grant from West Point to Appomattox*.

Over the course of more than seventeen years of research into Prang for various books, I have been privileged to correspond with experts, collectors, and dealers from across the country. Although I long ago lost contact with some of these people, I do wish to acknowledge their assistance and advice with appreciation, particularly Rachel Bolton, onetime marketing director of Hallmark Cards in Kansas City, Missouri; and Wally S. Beasley of Columbia, Tennessee, a Prang enthusiast who was generous enough to share with me reams of correspondence he had collected from the leaders of the Prang-Mark Society in upstate New York, and from dealers and Prang biographers from across the country.

I thank also the staff of the Civil War Institute at Gettysburg College, particularly its former student intern, Charles Dittrich, now a schoolteacher, for helping me find an important Prang newspaper review on the *HarpWeek* computer program.

I could never write any book about prints without noting with gratitude the many years

I have spent researching and writing on the subject of Civil War iconography in partnership with my good friend Mark E. Neely, Jr., the McCabe-Greer Professor of Civil War History at the Pennsylvania State University. He and I earlier tackled the Louis Prang theme together for our books *Mine Eyes Have Seen the Glory: The Civil War in Art* and, more recently, *The Union Image: Popular Prints of the Civil War North*. I do not doubt that he will find within this text some obvious debts to our earlier work.

And I am tremendously grateful to my executive assistant at the Metropolitan, Mary Jane Crook, who helped me so invaluably with all the details: correspondence, telephone calls, typing, and research—all, most generously, on her own time. Thank you, Mary Jane.

Most of all, I thank my wife, Edith, for patiently and usefully reading the manuscript, and encouraging me to complete it, literally between meals and during weekends that we might otherwise have spent at leisure. Later, she patiently proofread the computer-scanned printouts of the *Texts*, discovering countless errors that had eluded me and the machines alike. For me, this book marks a special way to celebrate our thirtieth wedding anniversary. I only hope she agrees.

From the beginning, Saverio Procario of Fordham University Press encouraged this project and backed it enthusiastically. Managing Editor Anthony Chiffolo and Production Manager Loomis Mayer guided its production at the Press and dealt patiently with the daunting task of adapting the Prang text into a computerized format. That effort required much work from many hands. Louis Prang, whose original chromos required similar commitment and labor from a host of specialists, would have been as impressed as I am grateful.

Rye, New York
January 1, 2001

# INTRODUCTION

## Louis Prang

### "PIONEER IN A GREAT FIELD"

It was Christmas Eve, 1864, but when President Abraham Lincoln sat down to open his daily mail, he found among the five hundred letters that had poured into the White House only a single holiday greeting. Just one piece of mail brought warm wishes for "a happy Christmas, health and success in your great labors." Appropriately enough, the sentiment came from the man who would go on to invent the Christmas card: Louis Prang (fig. 1).

The Boston-based picture publisher did not want to "bore" Lincoln "with a long letter expressing my high regard, my admiration," he wrote. Such support should be considered "a matter of course." Rather, the German-born printmaker

hoped that the beleaguered president might find "an hour of relaxation from your high duties" by examining what he had enclosed as a gift: an example of "what we here down east are doing in the Arts of peace to entertain the people, and at the same time to instruct and educate them."

Inside Prang's holiday package was an ornate album filled with "specimens of my own publications." These were most likely small, visiting-card–size lithographs depicting birds and flowers—what Prang liked to promote as his "beautiful art bits." All over the North, customers were eagerly buying these cards and placing them on display, along with photographs of their national leaders and loved ones, inside the

2

FIG. I.

Louis Prang, as he appeared in an undated photograph by F. Gutekunst of Philadelphia. *(Chicago Historical Society)*

leather family photograph albums that had grown immensely popular during the Civil War.

"I am fully conscious that what I have to send are mere trifles compared to the great achievements all around us," Prang continued, "and they might perhaps on that account be scarcely worthy [of] your attention." But, the image entrepreneur hastened to predict, "as the commencement of a comparatively new industry in this Country, as Pioneers in a great field to be cultivated they will claim some regard."[1]

By then, most of the country would have agreed on two counts: first, that prints had become extraordinarily popular and important to customers, who indeed held them in high "regard," even as Americans were consumed by the most tragic war of their history; and second, that Louis Prang of Boston had emerged as one of the most prominent pioneers in a great field.

This American pioneer was born in Breslau, Germany, on March 12, 1824. His father was a thriving calico printer there, and the elder Prang taught Louis to mix colors and print in color. By the time he was in his twenties, Louis had traveled throughout Europe on printing business and was beginning to achieve some success in the family enterprise. Fluent in French and English, he had fully mastered the calico trade as both an art and a science and had learned business techniques at a mercantile countinghouse in Westphalia.[2]

As historian Peter C. Marzio put it, Prang had with equal success "studied the accountant's book, the chemist's laboratory, the printer's ink bucket, and the common laborer's toil."[3] Looking ahead to the midpoint of the nineteenth century, Prang had every reason to believe that he was destined for success in his native land.

Politics intervened. A self-proclaimed "idealist," Prang became an activist in the upheavals that roiled Germany and much of Western Europe in 1848, working, he later remembered with undisguised pride, "to wrench freedom for a nation hungrey [*sic*] for it." He rose to become leader of a pro-democracy club in Herschberg, Silesia, but soon came to realize that opponents who, unlike him, were "satisfied with conditions" in the country were poised to march against the

3

---

1. Louis Prang to Lincoln, December 24, 1864, Abraham Lincoln Papers, Library of Congress. See also Harold Holzer, *Dear Mr. Lincoln: Letters to the President* (New York: Addison-Wesley, 1990), 226–27.

2. Sally Pierce and Catharina Slautterback, *Boston Lithography, 1825–1880: The Boston Athenaeum Collection* (Boston: The Boston Athenaeum, 1991), 148.

3. Peter C. Marzio, *The Democratic Art: Pictures for a 19th-century America* (Boston: David R. Godine, 1979), 98.

revolutionaries and to "prepare for us a chance for contemplation behind prison bars. Feeling conquered," Prang recalled, "I left with many others in the same predicerment [*sic*] to seek safety in other lands."[4]

At first, the young man found himself adrift and unsettled, migrating to Bohemia, then to Prague, and finally on to Zurich, before finally sailing from Le Havre for the United States in 1850. After docking in New York, he immediately headed north to Boston, where he spent the next six years working at various publishing jobs. Among the trades he tried were wood engraving and lithographic printing. Ultimately, publishing pictures seemed the most promising enterprise on the horizon, so he pursued it.

Prang found himself by the summer of 1856 "installed in a room about fifteen by eighteen, with one press, paper and stones which I had previously drawn and prepared for a plate of a simple bouquet of roses to be inserted as illustration in the Ladies' Companion of 1857." It was his key to success, "my first attempt at chromolithography," he remembered, "and although very unsatisfactory to me at the time, I look back on it with the fondness of a parent to his ever so homely child, as the starting point of that avalanche of color-work which subsequently rolled from my presses, and which gave my Boston establishment the reputation it now enjoys."[5]

Shortly thereafter, Prang began a short-lived partnership in Boston with fellow lithographer Julius Mayer (1833–1885). Prang & Mayer began publishing color-printed "chromos" in earnest, moving to Merchant's Row in 1858. Prang himself took responsibility for stone polishing and drawing. But by 1860, Prang was ready to expand on his own. He bought out his partner and established a new firm, which he named L. Prang & Co. By the outbreak of the Civil War, his single-press operation had grown into a factory boasting seven presses. The uncertain immigrant, who only a few years before had described himself almost schizophrenically as a "stonegrinder, draftsman, bookkeeper, and financial man all in one," was at last a well-established print publisher with an expanding company, a burgeoning reputation with the critics, and a growing audience.[6]

The Civil War helped make Prang a household name, for

---

4. Ibid., 97. The reminiscence comes from a hand-written, 155-page autobiography written by Prang around 1874, transcribed for a 1970 master's thesis by Mary Margaret Sittig, and quoted subsequently by Marzio.

5. Louis Prang, "Autobiographical Notes," typescript fragment in the Prints & Photographs Division, Library of Congress, Washington, D.C.

6. Pierce and Slautterback, *Boston Lithographers*, 148–49; Marzio, *The Democratic Art*, 98.

two reasons. On the one hand, it ignited demand for popular prints of war-related subjects: portraits of new military and civilian celebrities, and views of distant theaters of war. On the other, the conflict inspired a sentimental popular affection for peaceful genres, the picturesque "art bits" that suggested continuity and hope in the crucible of war. Prang was able to respond to both impulses and thrived.

Although he would not publish timely battle pictures as often or as quickly as the New York lithographers Currier & Ives—in fact, Prang never issued a true battle print of *any* kind while the war raged—he appeared content to sidestep this genre. Prang saw himself as an art publisher, not a news publisher. He would not simply respond to public demand. He would create it.

Novelty helped him find a niche in the growing market for cheap prints to decorate the home. Rival printmakers competed for audiences with war scenes and portraits designed to hang on the walls of that most sacred of domestic settings, the family parlor. There, such images testified to their owners' beliefs, in the manner of religious icons of old.[7]

Prang countered with small pictures for albums, and his business in these card-size prints boomed. *Harper's Weekly* observed of the publisher's decorative "art bits"—the very same prints he had sent to President Lincoln on December 24, 1864—that "Prang's various Albums and collections of colored prints of Leaves, Flowers, Scenes, and Children's Story-books, are furnished at so very moderate a price that they may be truly called Beauty for the Million. In the brilliant bewilderment of holiday selection he will not go wrong, and he will go very cheaply, who goes for Prang."[8] This was rare tribute: New York's leading pictorial weekly almost never commented editorially, much less favorably, about the work of other picture publishers.

As for his occasional display prints of the war itself, Prang's early efforts came in small and large sizes alike. Aware, as always, of the appeal of novelty, Prang became the first Northern lithographer to produce oversized, single-stone lithographic maps of the early seats of battlefield action. Prints like his *Harbor of Charleston with Fort Sumter* were issued on cheap newsprint and hawked on the street at newsstands or offered as a premium to newspaper subscribers. A similar early lithograph, *Maps of the Atlantic States, Forts Sumter, Pickens, Monroe*

5

7. On political prints as the successors to religious icons, see Robert Philippe, *Political Graphics: Art As a Weapon* (New York: Abbeville Press, 1980), 172.

8. *Harper's Weekly*, December 30, 1865.

*and McHenry*, featured a detailed plan of Washington, a sketch of Harpers Ferry, and a chart of distances and routes between major Northern and Southern cities. (The production might easily have served as a guide for an invading force, had Confederate generals only thought to purchase one!) Prominent, too, in this composition were portraits of Andrew Jackson, Abraham Lincoln, General Winfield Scott, and Sumter's hero, Major Robert Anderson. All of these pictures, texts, and charts were packed into one impressive, 20 x 26–inch broadside.[9]

Maps of Georgia, Bull Run, Atlanta, and Fortress Monroe eventually followed, along with a so-called "war telegram map." Prang went on to issue maps of the *Seacoast from Chesapeake Bay to Savannah Harbor; from Vicksburg to New Orleans*, and a map of the battles for Richmond during the ill-fated Peninsula Campaign of 1862.[10]

Although the early titles were rather plainly printed and offered rudimentary, hastily drawn portraiture, they did boast an appealing novelty: bold red blocks of color to highlight the spots where skirmishes and battles had been fought. And Prang came up with a clever marketing idea to promote these maps: he offered red and blue colored pencils with each so that buyers could themselves mark the tracks of the armies as they marched forward (or in some cases, retreated) in the weeks and months to come.[11]

For early enlistees and particularly for the families they left behind, Prang also published, early in the war, an ambitious 18 x 22–inch print entitled *Family Record/American Allegiance*. It prominently featured a solemn statement of loyalty to the Constitution and the government, along with a pledge (implicitly assumed by each of its purchasers) to defend both. The lithograph featured sentiments by George Washington, John Hancock, Thomas Jefferson, Lincoln, and even Lincoln's recent opponent in the race for the presidency, Stephen A. Douglas. A portrait of Washington crowned the composition, surrounded by likenesses of Lincoln and Generals Winfield Scott, Benjamin Butler, George McClellan, John C. Fremont, and John Wool, among others. This large, crowded testimonial to patriotism even cleverly offered blank space to encourage wives and parents to keep a personal record of their own family members' service in the Union Army.

---

9. Katherine Morrison McClinton, *The Chromolithographs of Louis Prang* (New York: Clarkson N. Potter, 1973), 141.

10. Larry Freeman, *Louis Prang: Color Lithographer* (Watkins Glen, N.Y.: Century House, 1971), 31.

11. Ibid., 26.

FIG. 2.

A. Kipps, after a photograph by Alexander Hesler, *Abraham Lincoln.* Published by L. Prang & Co., Boston, 1861. Lithograph, 6 x 7 7/8 inches. This was the third version of the Kipps lithograph to be published by Prang: the first was a straight-forward adaptation of Hesler's 1857 photograph, with Lincoln's hair neatened a bit; the second, issued in hasty response to the subject's decision to grow a beard, erroneously showed him in muttonchop side-whiskers; and this final version, which imposed a full beard in an attempt to bring the picture up to date. *(The Lincoln Museum, Fort Wayne, Indiana; neg. no. 2286)*

Prang also tried tapping the robust market for Lincoln portraits—but with nothing approaching the frenzied response that propelled rival printmakers in Chicago, New York, Philadelphia, and his own Boston. His initial effort, in fact, was a ludicrous attempt to update a beardless, A. K. Kipps campaign lithograph (fig. 2) by superimposing uncharacteristically thick whiskers that looked little like the beard the president-elect had begun to grow after his election. It no doubt initially fooled an audience unfamiliar with the new president's new appearance, but its rarity today suggests that it was not a best-seller in 1861. For the next four years, Prang steered clear of the potentially lucrative Lincoln field.[12]

The printmaker fared much better with smaller Civil War prints created to be collected and displayed in albums. Notably, he issued a set of lithographic portraits in *carte-de-visite* size, constituting a virtual pictorial who's who of the military elite serving "under the Union flag," as advertisements for it boasted. A New York printmaker named Elias Dexter undertook a similar project, which boasted decidedly more handsome results: finished-looking portraits with dark backgrounds that seemed almost photographic in appearance. By contrast, Prang's rival offerings may have looked more like sketches, but he boldly advertised them as "executed in superior line engraving." Heavily promoted, they proved astonishingly popular, issued in individual sizes for family albums, in groupings suitable for framing, and in "book form with hard stamped covers." The price was a reasonable thirty cents for each set of twenty-four pictures.[13]

Advertising his firm in the 1862 *Boston Almanac*, Prang listed all of his specialties (maps, bill heads, show cards, plans, and views) but took pains to identify his firm as "publishers of the well-known *Card Portraits* [*carte-de-visite*–size lithographic portraits of Union officers and other celebrities], Maps, Pictures, and the *Family Record of American Allegiance*, which no loyal family should be without."[14]

Prang expanded his Civil War card inventory to include both comic and sentimental depictions of war—that is, the "war" that his artists observed from behind the lines. For two of these series he hired a frustrated but ambitious young painter named Winslow Homer, who had only recently escaped what he called

12. See Harold Holzer, Gabor S. Boritt, and Mark E. Neely, Jr., *The Lincoln Image: Abraham Lincoln and the Popular Print* (New York: Scribner's, 1984), 74.

13. McClinton, *Chromolithographs of Louis Prang*, 72, 141.
14. Pierce and Slautterback, *Boston Lithographers*, 148.

the "bondage" and "slavery" of apprenticeship to a rival Boston lithographer, J. H. Bufford. Homer had already been south to the Virginia front to cover the war up close as a so-called "special" artist for *Harper's Weekly;* now in 1863 he agreed to return to printmaking and work for Prang.

Their first project was an ambitious, six-plate portfolio offering 11 x 14–inch black-and-white lithographs of camp life. To facilitate Homer's work, Prang evidently sent directly to his peripatetic artist some heavy, pre-polished lithographic stones, ready to receive their crayoned images. By December, 1863, Homer wrote to Boston to assure his publisher: "The stone was received all right. I shall commence it very soon, probably send it to you week from Wednesday." The skillful results were entitled *Campaign Sketches* and were offered to the public by the set for $1.50.[15]

The series offered some intricate and intoxicating work that was designed to evoke both laughter and longing: a scene of eager soldiers lining up at a campfire to await *The Coffee Call;* an attentive female volunteer helping a bedridden, wounded soldier compose *The Letter for Home;* a group of soldiers engaged in the illicit *Pass Time* of card-playing (fig. 3); two harried soldiers trying desperately to capture a cow from enraged field workers in *Foraging* (fig. 4); and a stereotypical portrait of *Our Jolly Cook,* presenting a caricatured African American servant entertaining the soldiers by dancing merrily at the campfire. Homer's haunting cover illustration (fig. 5) may have been the best work in the entire portfolio: a contemplative, back-lit portrait of a lone common soldier, knapsack on his back, toting his rifle as he saunters toward the viewer—and toward his unforseeable destiny.[16]

Homer was delighted with the portfolio. "The cover is very neat," he told Prang, "and the pictures look better than they would in color." Just in time for Christmas, 1864—around the same time he sent his "art bits" to President Lincoln—Prang proudly advertised the set in New York: "Campaign Sketches. — Designed and drawn on stone by Winslow Homer. A series of spirited Camp scenes sketched on the spot by Mr. Homer and executed in high artistic style in crayon. These sketches are sold in sets of 6 copies and put up in a neat cover." But per-

---

15. Nicolai Cikovsky, Jr., and Franklin Kelly, *Winslow Homer* (New Haven, Conn.: Yale University Press, 1993), 393; McClinton, *Chromolithographs of Louis Prang,* 67–70; Lloyd Goodrich, *The Graphic Art of Winslow Homer* (New York: Museum of Graphic Art, 1968), 10.

16. See Mark E. Neely, Jr., and Harold Holzer, *The Union Image: Popular Prints of the Civil War North* (Chapel Hill, N.C.: University of North Carolina Press, 2000), 69.

10

FIG. 3.

Winslow Homer, *A Pass Time*. Published by L. Prang & Co., Boston, 1861. Lithograph, 14 x 10⅞ inches. One of the six prints from the Civil War portfolio *Campaign Sketches*, this night scene shows soldiers lounging around a smoky campfire, playing cards. The man standing at left, holding a sword, may be a sentry who has thoughtlessly abandoned his post to observe the game. Civil War military chaplains spent much time preaching against gambling, to little avail. *(Museum of Fine Arts, Boston; Gift of Charles G. Loring)*

FIG. 4.

Winslow Homer, *Foraging*. Published by L. Prang & Co., Boston, 1861. Lithograph, 14 x 10⁷/₈ inches, signed lower left: *Homer Del.* Another entry from *Campaign Sketches*, this amusing picture depicts a trio of soldiers trying to capture their dinner from a Virginia farm. Armed comrades in the background stand guard over the theft, but one field worker (right) raises his arms upright in outrage. Sick of bad rations, soldiers occasionally defied orders and foraged on livestock at nearby farms. *(Museum of Fine Arts, Boston; Gift of Charles G. Loring)*

12

FIG. 5.

Winslow Homer, cover art for *Campaign Sketches*, *Del. and Drawn on Stone by Winslow Homer*. Published by L. Prang & Co., Boston. Lithograph, 14 x 10⅞ inches. The illustrated title page for the 1861 Homer-Prang collaboration offered the best image in the entire portfolio, a beautifully rendered depiction of a lone soldier walking toward the viewer. *Campaign Sketches* remained on sale by Prang until at least 1868. *(Prang's Chromo, January 1868). (Museum of Fine Arts, Boston; Gift of Charles G. Loring)*

haps the portfolio did not sell as well as the artist and publisher had hoped. The original set was issued as "Part 1," but no subsequent edition ever appeared.[17]

Instead, Prang next asked Homer to create a more informal set of comic and sentimental pictures, called *Life in Camp*. The series appeared in two editions, each featuring twelve small chromolithographed cards suitable for mounting in photo albums. Each set of a dozen was priced at fifty cents. Prang paid his artist all of $80 for his efforts (figs. 6, 7).[18]

Individual scenes featured such informed, behind-the-lines observations as *The Field Barber* giving a skeptical soldier a haircut; a fetching portrait of a comely woman entitled *The Girl He Left Behind*; and a soldier *Home on Furlough*, enthusiastically applauding a theatrical production from a first-row box seat. Humorous titles included *Hard Tack*, in which a soldier struggles to chew a hilariously oversized piece of indigestible rations; *A Shell is Coming*, depicting two privates cowering fearfully behind a tree; and *An Unwelcome Visit*, in which an intrusive mule sends a tent collapsing down on two sleeping recruits. Homer would later expand some of these very ideas into formal oil paintings: *The Guard House*, for example, in which a miscreant soldier is made to stand for hours on a barrel, would become the acclaimed painting *Punishment for Intoxication*.[19]

Homer moved on to tackle the war theme on canvas, but Prang persevered with his modest but unique Civil War prints. One particularly good effort was the large, 14 x 24–inch, three-color 1862 lithograph, possibly the work of Boston printmaker Benjamin B. Russell, which offered a *View of the Stone Fleet which Sailed from New Bedford November 15th 1861* (fig. 8). It was the only known print depiction of the armada of idle whaling vessels that had been purchased by the federal navy, loaded with granite, and sent to Charleston Harbor in South Carolina. There, the ships were scuttled to plug up the harbor and deter blockade running. The scheme failed because the old hulks rotted away within months.[20]

**13**

---

17. *New York Tribune*, December 17, 1864; Goodrich, *Graphic Art of Winslow Homer*, 10.

18. Originals in the collection of The Metropolitan Museum of Art. See also Neely and Holzer, *Union Image*, 70, 72–73; for Homer's fee see Gordon Hendricks, *The Life and Work of Winslow Homer* (New York: Harry N. Abrams, 1960), n.p., quoting original letter in the Museum of Fine Arts, Boston.

19. Harold Holzer and Mark E. Neely, Jr., *Mine Eyes Have Seen the Glory: The Civil War in Art* (New York: Orion Books, 1993), 297. The original of the painting is in the Canajoharie Library and Art Gallery in Canajoharie, New York.

20. Robert K. Newman, ed., The Old Print Shop *Portfolio* 59, 124; on the Stone Fleets (of which the armada Prang depicted was but one), see Patricia L. Faust, ed., *Historical Times Illustrated Encyclopedia of the Civil War* (New York: Harper & Row, 1986), 720.

FIG. 6.

Winslow Homer, *Life in Camp*, first set of twelve 4 x 2⅜–inch cards mounted on an album page, 13¾ x 12½ inches. From top row, left, the cards depicted: a worker building a fortification *In the Trenches*; a sad *Good Bye*; soldiers *Fording* a stream; a Zouave roasting his *Extra Ration*, a pig; *The Field Barber* giving a recruit a haircut; *The Girl He Left Behind*; a *Drummer*; a *Deserter*; *Home on a Furlough*; a determined defender in *The Rifle Pit*; a rear view of a *Teamster* and his caravan of supplies; and *Our Special*, an artist who looked like a cross between Thomas Nast and Homer himself. (*The Metropolitan Museum of Art; Gift of Jefferson R. Burdick*, 1947)

FIG. 7.

Winslow Homer, *Life in Camp*, second set of chromo cards. More comic in tone, this set of a dozen cards showed, from top left: a soldier *Building Castles* with the smoke from his pipe; a disgusted recruit struggling to eat *Hard Tack*; a clumsy soldier who has *Upset His Coffee*; a soldier about to be tossed into a stream for an unexpected *Water Call*; soldiers hiding in the trees when *A Shell Is Coming*; soldiers having fun (and probably experiencing pain) *Riding on a Rail*; shirkers lining up for *A Surgeon's Call* (a scene Homer later adapted into a formal painting); *An Unwelcome Visit* by a stray mule; soldiers racing out of their tents, *Late for Roll Call*; a hapless marcher *Stuck in the Mud*; punishment as meted out in an ersatz *Guard House*; and more camp frolics in *Tossing in a Blanket*. (*The Metropolitan Museum of Art; Gift of Jefferson R. Burdick, 1947*)

15

16

FIG. 8.

Benjamin Russell, *View of the Stone Fleet which Sailed from New Bedford Nov. 16th 1861*. Published by L. Prang & Co., Boston, 1862. Chromolithograph, 13⁹/₁₆ x 24⁷/₈ inches. In 1861 the Federal navy purchased fifteen idle whaleships in New Bedford, loaded them with granite, sailed them into the Confederacy, and then sent the vessels to the bottom off Charleston, South Carolina, to plug up the harbor and inhibit blockade running. This print portrayed the fleet as a handsome armada. The caption information identified each ship by name, provided the name of the ships' captains, and noted the precise number of stones and tonnage each carried south. *(The Old Print Shop, New York)*

VIEW OF THE STONE FLEET WHICH SAILED FROM NEW BEDFORD NOV. 16TH 1861.

At least once, Prang also rather daringly produced a portrait of a Confederate celebrity, *Captain Semmes of the Pirate "Alabama."* Depictions of "enemy" officers were rare from this, or any other, Northern print publisher once the war effectively cut off the Southern sales market. Union audiences doubtless resented, and perhaps even boycotted, such efforts. There is no record of how the Semmes print was received. We know only that until peace was restored Prang offered no further depictions of Confederates. Not for a quarter of a century would he return to the theme of the *Alabama* for his famous Civil War chromo series.

From quite the opposite perspective, L. Prang & Co. in 1861 co-published lithographer Dominique Fabronious's ornate pictorial plea for abolition, *The American Declaration of Independence Illustrated* (fig. 9). The print showed a well-dressed freedman and a newly unshackled slave rising into the air from inside a sort of hot-air balloon basket, lifted aloft by an American eagle as crowds of whites cheer from below and slogans proclaim, "All Men are Created Equal" and "Break Every Yoke! Let the oppressed go free!" There is nothing quite like this print in the entire Prang catalogue—but since its caption reveals that it was co-copyrighted by Thayer & Co., another Boston firm, Prang's participation may have been limited merely to the loaning out of his printing presses.[21]

Yet another unique Prang effort of the period constituted his only campaign cartoon for the 1864 presidential election, a campaign that inspired scores of caricatures from other printmakers. Prang's sole contribution was *Democracy 1832, 1864* (fig. 10). It contrasted Andrew Jackson's firm response to secession advocate John C. Calhoun thirty-two years earlier, with Democratic presidential nominee George B. McClellan's alleged capitulation to Confederate President Jefferson Davis during the current political campaign. Here was a decidedly pro-Lincoln print without a specific mention or depiction of Lincoln—but effective, certainly, as character assassination against the Union general now seeking the White House on a peace platform.

Notwithstanding this fascinating body of work, it would be entirely misleading to suggest that L. Prang & Co. focused exclusively, or even principally, on Civil War subjects from 1861 to 1865. Quite the contrary was true. The firm continued producing genre scenes, portraits, and "sentimentals"

---

21. Bernard F. Reilly, Jr., *American Political Prints: 1776–1876—A Catalogue of the Collection in the Library of Congress* (Boston: G. K. Hall, 1991), 484–85.

FIG. 9.

Dominique Fabronious, *The American Declaration of Independence Illustrated*. Published by Thayer & Co. and L. Prang & Co., Boston, 1861. Lithograph, 18¹⁄₂ x 13 inches. Perhaps issued as a premium for subscribers to the *Boston Herald* (a newsboy hawking that paper can be seen among the crowd in the foreground), this abolitionist print linked the cause of freedom directly to the promise of equality in the Declaration of Independence. The verses accompanying the picture declare: "A man is a man howe'er dark his skin, / A heart that is human is beating within, / God regards not his color—and neither should we, / Then 'unchain' the Negro— and let him go free." *(Library of Congress)*

FIG. 10.

L. Prang & Co., *Democracy. 1832. 1864.* Boston, 1864. Lithograph, 10¼ x 15 inches. Prang's only known pictorial comment on the 1864 presidential campaign, this two-panel cartoon shows (left) an earlier, Democratic general-turned-president, Andrew Jackson, denouncing John C. Calhoun's anti-Unionism back in 1832. By contrast, George B. McClellan, the Democratic general who was running for the White House in 1864 (right), is shown groveling before Confederate President Jefferson Davis, clutching an olive branch, ready for "peace" even if it means "friendly separation." *(The Lincoln Museum, Fort Wayne, Indiana, neg. no. 2980)*

20

throughout the war years, and the variety and sheer number of published titles suggest that Prang found a ready audience for nonmilitary lithographs.

The Library of Congress in Washington, D.C., the most comprehensive repository of nineteenth-century popular prints in the nation, owns some 226 individually catalogued Prang lithographs, along with several boxes of proof pictures and long-forgotten additional folders of florals, Boston city views, religious images, Central Park scenes, animal and bird prints, countless Christmas and Valentine's Day designs, and even a group of unintentionally hilarious so-called "society pictures" showing amorous or quarreling young lovers watched over by chubby cupids. The Boston Public Library, which holds the largest public Prang collection in the nation, owns many of the firm's scenes, portraits, sheet music covers, and genre chromos.

Prang's prolific output included portrayals of the game of baseball, many depictions of exotic scenery in distant California, cloying genre scenes bearing titles like *Baby in Trouble*, *Children's Picnic*, *Playing Mother*, and *Our Pet Polly*, and a series of occupational pictures entitled *Prang's Aids for Object Teaching*, which were supposed to inspire young people into useful career choices through portrayals of hard-working black-

smiths, carpenters, farmers, shoemakers, tinsmiths, and, of course, lithographers (fig. 11).

Supplementing this catalogue of sugary pictures, which were clearly aimed at rural and rather simple tastes, Prang offered ambitious, color-printed adaptations of famous paintings, Prang's favorite kind of work; these were all squarely designed for the middle-class home. By 1869 the chief arbiters of domestic taste, Harriet Beecher Stowe and Catherine Ward Beecher, would specifically recommend to housewives three "really admirable pictures of some of our best American artists." All were products of L. Prang & Co.: Eastman Johnson's *Barefoot Boy* for $5, Henry Roderick Newman's *Blue-Fringed Gentians* for $6, and Albert Bierstadt's *Sunset in the Yosemite Valley* for $12. "These chromos," the Beechers enthused, were truly worthy of the most "economical, healthful, beautiful and Christian homes." Over the next thirty years, Prang would issue some eight hundred chromo copies of oil and watercolor originals, the vast majority of them peaceful American subjects.[22]

---

22. Catherine E. Beecher and Harriet Beecher Stowe, *The American Woman's Home, or Principles of Domestic Science . . .* (Hartford, Conn.: Stowe-Day Foundation, 1994 reprint of 1869 edition), title page, 91–92; Prang's output cited in Marzio, *Democratic Art*, 102–3.

FIG. 11.

L. Prang & Co., *Lithographer*. Boston, 1874. Lithograph, 13 x 17 inches. One of *Prang's Aids for Object Teaching*, designed to promote useful "trades and occupations," this celebration of Prang's own industry also provided a rare behind-the-scenes look at the inner workings of his "printory." A "finisher" can be seen working on an image at left; a copyist sits before the window working to reproduce an oil painting; and printers labor at the steam presses in the background. *(Library of Congress)*

22

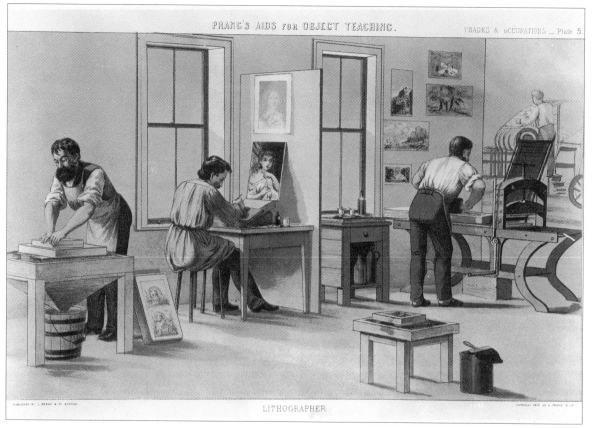

PRANG'S AIDS FOR OBJECT TEACHING.

TRADES & OCCUPATIONS _ Plate 5.

LITHOGRAPHER.

But Prang could not easily afford to ignore the Civil War altogether, especially after it ended. As soon as peace was restored in April, 1865, the owners of many "Christian homes" seemed more eager than ever to include among their decorations affordable pictures that recalled the sacrifices and the leaders that had preserved the Union.

Prang was neither swift nor particularly prolific in his initial response. When, for example, in the wake of Lincoln's death, his competitors in New York and Boston rushed out assassination and deathbed scenes, along with reverential portraits of the new national martyr, Prang weighed into this hungry marketplace but cautiously. He merely supplied one of the many unremarkable 1865 print adaptations of Mathew Brady's famous studio photograph of Lincoln and his son, Tad, looking at a large book. With far more originality, Prang later adapted an 1860 photograph of a clean-shaven Lincoln standing in the front yard of his house in Springfield, Illinois, into a handsome lithograph entitled *Home of Abraham Lincoln*. For its caption, Prang added two lines of well-crafted tribute that poignantly recalled the Lincoln who had posed on his doorstep only five years earlier on the verge of national crisis and immortality: "He left it in peace, to preside over a nation then in bondage. / He now reposes under its soil a martyr to the Freedom he won."

The most notable Lincoln portrait to come from Prang's presses in this period was his superb lithograph of the last painting ever made of the president from life. Although Connecticut artist Matthew Wilson had painted the original on commission for Secretary of the Navy Gideon Welles, Wilson subsequently made a copy expressly for Prang's use, completing it in May, 1865. The resulting lithographic adaptation (fig. 12) proved not only the last Lincoln print based on a life portrait but one of the first ambitious post-assassination Lincoln prints as well. On Lincoln and the Civil War themes, Prang was thus able to make up in quality for what his catalogue lacked in quantity.[23]

The Wilson adaptation may also rank as Prang's last great hurrah in the field of black-and-white printmaking, certainly as far as Civil War subjects were concerned. He now began devoting himself more passionately than ever to full-time, full-color work. Writing to the printmaker years later to defend the use of black-and-white in prints, Homer insisted, "What you say about the lith tint being the best means of expression for an artist I cannot agree with you." But Prang remained unconvinced. He was determined to recall the battles and

---

23. Holzer, Boritt, and Neely, *Lincoln Image*, 142–44.

24

FIG. 12.

L. Prang & Co., after Matthew Wilson, *Abraham Lincoln. Copied by permission from the original picture by Matthew Wilson—now in possession of Hon. Gideon Welles, Secretary of the Navy.* Boston, 1865. Lithograph with tintstone, 14$^{7}$/$_{8}$ x 18 inches. When he saw the finished painting on which this print was based, Lincoln reportedly joked that it looked "horridly like" the original. This handsome adaptation, based in part (as was the original painting) on an Alexander Gardner photograph, appeared just in time to reach audiences hungry for authentic portraits of the assassinated president. *(The Lincoln Museum, Fort Wayne, Indiana, neg. no. 2313)*

heroes of the Civil War by using the color-printing processes he had mastered so well.[24]

His business grew exponentially. By 1867, Prang had expanded his enterprise into a "printory"—the word he coined for his print factory—housing dozens of busy presses. He returned with a vengeance to what he called "my old love—the printing in color," particularly "the ideal work which I never lost sight of, the reproduction of oil and water color paintings." Prang was well prepared for this adventure. While the war was still raging in 1864, he had sailed to Europe for a firsthand tour of its leading lithography operations. He returned home to Boston armed with ideas for new techniques and within three years was focusing enthusiastically and almost exclusively on color printing. He was now sure he could produce chromos that looked very much like original paintings and sell them at affordable prices to American audiences. By the end of 1868, Prang had produced no fewer than forty-six examples and had launched a self-promoting quarterly publication entitled *Prang's Chromo: A Journal of Popular Art*, which he offered for free. Yet for years more, the Civil War remained for him a great theme waiting to be tackled.[25]

The closest he initially got to the subject after 1865 was a portrait of former General Ulysses S. Grant, published just in time to boost the Union hero's candidacy for president in 1868. It was offered in black-and-white for twenty-five cents and in color for fifty cents. Also in 1868, Prang paid artist Eastman Johnson the princely sum of $700 for the rights to issue a chromo of his canvas *The Boyhood of Lincoln*, an inspirational scene showing the future president reading by firelight in his prairie log cabin.[26]

Two years later, the firm issued a handsome chromo portrait of Hiram Revels (fig. 13), the Reconstruction-era African American senator who occupied Jefferson Davis's old seat from Mississippi. The great black leader Frederick Douglass usefully praised the print as "a faithful representation of the man" and urged former slaves to purchase it. "I think the walls of their houses will soon begin to bear evidence of their altered relations to the people about them," Douglass predicted. Prang's audience was growing. But the printmaker's response to the Civil War remained sluggish.[27]

Finally, in 1870, the printmaker found a Civil War painting

---

24. Homer to Prang, November 22, 1895, original in the Archives of American Art, Washington, D.C.

25. Marzio, *Democratic Art*, 98–103.

26. *Prang's Chromo*, January 1868; Marzio, *Democratic Art*, 95, 320. Original of the Johnson chromo is in the Print Department of the Boston Public Library.

27. Ibid., 104.

26

FIG. 13.

L. Prang & Co., after Theodore Kaufmann, *Hon. H. R. Revels*. Boston, 1870. Chromolithograph, 14 x 11³/₄ inches. Prang promoted this print as an "exact imitation of an Oil Painting, and hardly to be distinguished from it." It depicted the first elected African American U.S. Senator, Hiram Revels of Mississippi. Frederick Douglass remarked of it bluntly: "We colored men so often see ourselves described and painted as monkeys, that we think it a great piece of good fortune to find an exception to this general rule." (*The New National Era* [October 20, 1870]:3; Katherine M. McClinton, *The Chromolithographs of Louis Prang*, 37). (*Library of Congress*)

he deemed worthy of reproduction as part of his popular series of "Prang's American Chromos." He issued a chromolithograph of Theodore Kaufmann's canvas *Lashed to the Shrouds—Farragut Passing the Forts at Mobile, In his Flagship Hartford* (fig. 14), showing Admiral David G. Farragut in the rigging of the Union warship during the Battle of Mobile Bay on August 5, 1864. That day, Farragut had courageously insisted that he be tied to the rigging of his ship so that he might continue to command his fleet even if wounded in the fierce fighting. Kaufmann's depiction failed to capture the drama or sweep of the smoky engagement, but for Prang it represented an important, if tentative, first step toward chromolithography designed specifically to evoke Civil War memories.[28]

At last, Prang seemed to recognize the yearning for such pictures. In 1873 he issued an adaptation (fig. 15) of artist Julian Scott's composition *Sold!* (sometimes known as *Fooled!*). It showed a group of Union soldiers overrunning an enemy entrenchment, only to discover that the "soldiers" who had been keeping them at bay were nothing more than decoys "armed" with mock wooden guns, set up by wily Confederates to deceive the federals.[29] Precisely why Prang turned to this particularly frustrating, decidedly unheroic scene, or why he never again worked in partnership with talented painter Scott, remains a mystery. Again, Prang was still merely dipping a toe in the artistic waters of Civil War recollection. Not for another fifteen years would he make a triumphant reentry to the genre with the ambitious portfolio that finally allowed him to unite his determination to reproduce original art with his recognition of the intense public interest in a war that had once divided the country and still dominated its thoughts.

By this time, L. Prang & Co. confidently billed itself as "Art & Education Publishers," specializing in chromos of Americana, landscapes, birds and animals, farm and home scenes, still lifes, biblical and religious pictures, drawing-room pictures, album cards, and, perhaps most prominently of all, greeting cards, all of which could be "ordered through any Art Dealer or Bookseller in the U. S. or Canada or Directly from us." He established himself on Roxbury Street and built a fine home for himself in back of his factory.[30]

---

28. That same year, Prang also issued Kaufmann's manual, *American Painting Book: The Art of Painting or of Imitating the Effects of Color in Nature* (Boston: L. Prang & Co., 1871).

29. The original canvas was entitled *Confederate Decoys*. See Robert J. Titterton, *Julian Scott: Artist of the Civil War* (Jefferson, N.C.: McFarland & Co., 1997), 98, opp. 117.

30. L. Prang & Co., *An Illustrated Catalogue of Art Publications for 1873;* Pierce and Slautterback, *Boston Lithography,* 149. Prang actually built the house first, then erected a factory nearby.

28

FIG. 14.

L. Prang & Co., after Theodore Kaufmann, *Lashed to the Shrouds. Farragut Passing the Forts at Mobile in his Flagship, the Hartford.* Boston, 1870. Chromolithograph, 20 x 16 inches. Clutching a spyglass and tied about the waist to the rigging of his battleship, Admiral David Glasgow Farragut commands his fleet at the Battle of Mobile Bay in 1864. This image, one of "Prang's American Chromos," suffered from an uninspired design that failed to convey the high drama of that fierce naval encounter. But unlike most portraits of Farragut, who was sixty-three at the time, it did little to disguise his age. *(Library of Congress)*

FIG. 15.

L. Prang & Co., after Julian Scott, *Sold!* Boston, 1870. Chromolithograph, 20 x 16 inches. Shocked Federal troops storm a Confederate entrenchment, only to find that the "battery" that had been holding them at bay was comprised of logs, not cannon, and "defended" by scarecrow-like decoys, not soldiers. Scott tried to show surprise, shame, and anger on the faces of the Union troops, one of whom (right) peers into the distance in search of the real enemy, who have presumably set up the elaborate hoax to mask their retreat. Note that the fleeing Confederates have left a canteen and playing cards on the ground in their haste to escape. *(Library of Congress)*

Many sources credit Prang with inventing the Christmas card, and he was the first to agree. At the very least, he marketed greeting cards into a national obsession, in part by suggesting loftily that they "schooled people to appreciate the beautiful and taught them to expect something of a higher order of merit." More to the point, the printmaker understood that "the vast mass of the population is reached through the heart," and his greeting cards, whether for Christmas or Valentine's Day, invariably featured "cooing birds . . . tender maids or sheepish lovers," and maudlin "home scenes" of motherhood and infancy. The results sold in the millions.[31]

Prang also strove to ensure that his efforts were taken seriously. He exhibited original greeting-card drawings at art exhibitions and once mounted a $2,000 competition for the best card design. When a well-regarded illustrator won the $500 first prize, the *New York Evening Post* rhapsodized: "It is easy to see that art is advancing in this country when Elihu Vedder makes our Christmas cards." Critics (and there were many), who dismissed Prang's best-sellers as "airy nothings" and warned that they threatened to corrupt American taste, remained in the minority.[32]

By the Gilded Age of the 1880s, a visitor entering Prang's rebuilt, expanded 286 Roxbury Street factory (the original building had been destroyed by fire) would find eight power presses and eighteen hand presses busily at work, with scores of employees laboring away on stones, applying inks, and "finishing" pictures. A critic from nearby Lowell observed the scene in 1885:

Entering the office one steps at once into an atmosphere of art. Some of the more striking and recent productions of the house are displayed on the counters; a frame of medals won in scores of exhibitions attract [*sic*] this idea; on the long table are albums devoted to the cards and pictures which form so extensive a feature of the firm's catalogue. Sometimes chromos and the oil paintings from which they were taken are hung side by side in identical frames. So close are the reproductions that often even the artist could not tell which was brush and which was printing press.[33]

---

31. *The American Spectator* 20 (December 30, 1886):1005; *The Art Age* 1 (April 1884):94.

32. Luna Lambert, *The Seasonal Trade: Holiday Gift and Greeting Cards* (Washington, D.C.: Smithsonian Institution Press, 1982), [5–13].

33. *Lowell Daily Courier*, May 5, 1885, quoted in McClinton, *Chromolithographs of Louis Prang*, 21. The Prang factory is long gone, but a small "Prang Street," located between the back entrance of the Museum of Fine Arts and the esplanade leading to the Isabella Gardner Museum, today runs not far from where the original building once stood. See also *Atlas of the City of Boston: Proper and Roxbury* (Philadelphia: G. W. Bromley & Co., 1890), Plate 25.

Indeed, Prang prided himself on his faithful attention to artistic detail, although he was careful to remind audiences that his goal was copying, not producing, original art. "Chromo-lithography is in itself an art to reproduce, to imitate, not to create," he maintained, explaining, "Chromo-lithography is for the painting what the type is to the writer."[34]

Yet he was about to commission the most ambitious retrospective pictorial series ever conceived to portray the Civil War. The firm of Kurz & Allison, Prang's competitors in Chicago, had launched a series of their own in 1884 (or, more precisely, had issued a *Battle of Gettysburg* chromo that year to such acclaim that they produced three more battle scenes in 1886, another three in 1887, and seven more in 1888, ultimately producing thirty-six Civil War prints by 1894). Their chromos were highly popular, but no one could have mistaken them for fine art. Chalky-looking, repetitive in design, and occasionally inaccurate, they aimed to replicate in miniature the scope and sweep of battle cycloramas without aspiring, as Prang did, to bring true art to the masses.[35]

Precisely how Prang hit upon the idea to produce his own portfolio of Civil War chromos is lost to history. But once he decided to do so, he spared neither attention nor expense. Not satisfied merely to copy previously existing originals (including Homer's later triumphs, perhaps because they showed life in camp, not on the battlefield), he commissioned military artist Thure de Thulstrup to produce twelve new portrayals of land battles and hired marine artist Julian Oliver Davidson to create original watercolor depictions of six naval battles. These would then be chromolithographed and issued as a comprehensive portfolio. Records are incomplete, but Thulstrup is known to have received handsome fees: $250, $457.75, and $400 for three of his watercolors. Davidson was paid between $300 and $375 for the original models that he supplied for the series. A promotional flyer would later maintain that L. Prang & Co. spent $30,000 in all to research, commission, manufacture, and promote the prints.[36]

Prang's stated goal, his catalogues proclaimed, was to produce pictures "for the enjoyment of the masses and the spread of art-education." But promotional literature for the new Civil

---

34. Larry Freeman, *Louis Prang: Color Lithographer, Giant of a Man* (Watkins Glen, N.Y.: Century House, 1971), 85.

35. Neely and Holzer, *Union Image*, 212–14.

36. Charlotte Adams, *Catalogue of unusual collection of water-colors and oil paintings purchased . . . by L. Prang & Co.* (New York: American Art Association), 3, 5, 77, 81. Original in the print collection, New York Public Library; McClinton, *Chromolithographs of Louis Prang*, 237. Thulstrup received the $400 fee for his watercolor model of the Battle of Shiloh.

War series took pains to herald its special appeal to veterans and their children. The chromos would be "worthy, from the rare quality of their artistic execution, to a place in the best collections of American art, as well as in the homes, whether rich or humble, of the surviving heroes of the War, or their descendants." Proclaimed the company's brochure: "The illustrated press, the patriotic portraiture, and the episodic pictures of the war had fostered the popular taste for pictorialism. The American nation now wanted pictures. It should have them." It would be "a series of exquisitely beautiful Facsimile Prints, rendered in the highest style of modern art." And to produce the models on which they would be based, Prang promised to use "masterly original paintings by the most famous living American artists."[37]

Swedish-born Thulstrup, known to his friends as "Thully," had served in the French army, migrated to America, and first worked for Prang in 1873, preparing maps for an atlas. He went on to contribute drawings to several illustrated newspapers in New York, eventually joining the staff of *Harper's Weekly*, with which he remained associated for thirty-five years. According to Thulstrup authority Steven E. Smith, the artist earned a reputation "as a master of the crowd scene" and became *Harper's* "leading illustrator of important public events." A former artillery officer and civil engineer, he also began in 1884 to contribute drawings for the *Century Magazine*'s hugely successful series *Battles and Leaders of the Civil War*. Both Prang and Kurz & Allison were undoubtedly influenced by the popularity of this series, and it was only natural that Prang would turn to one of its illustrators to provide models for the chromos that he decided to issue himself in 1886. Once he hired him, Prang immediately proclaimed Thulstrup "the foremost military artist of America," and eventually, critics followed suit. At the artist's death in 1930, Thulstrup's "famous battle scenes" would be lauded as "some of the most familiar scenes of American life now extant."[38]

Davidson, too, had contributed to *Battles and Leaders*, which, by the time Prang commissioned his Civil War chromos, was

---

37. McClinton, *Chromolithographs of Louis Prang*, 151; Freeman, *Louis Prang*, 87; *Prospectus. Prang's War Pictures. Aquarelle Facsimile Prints.* (Boston: L. Prang & Co., 1887), original in the Print Collection, Boston Public Library.

38. Steven E. Smith, "Thure de Thulstrup: Harper's Workhorse," *Imprint* 21 (August 1996):2–8; *New York Times* (June 10, 1930); *Prang War Pictures. Set of Twenty Were $80.00. A Few Now at $20.00.* Advertisement of the Historical Art Company, Boston, in *Current History* 10 (April 2000):20; *Prang's War Pictures* (1888 Prospectus).

destined for republication, and even broader impact, in book form. (It would appear in 1888.[39]) Born in 1853, Davidson had gone to sea at age eighteen and then studied art under the accomplished marine painter Mauritz F. H. DeHaas. Several of his naval scenes had already been engraved for *Harper's Weekly* and were universally judged, a Boston newspaper reported, "to be standard works of their kind." Exhibiting in New York as early as 1872, Davidson was known for panoramic perspective and technical acumen, talents he would bring to the Prang project the following decade. The Boston printmaker, describing his marine artist as "much admired," was aiming high.[40]

In fact, Prang's series would not offer mere chromos but, as he touted them, "aquarelle facsimile prints," a fancy-sounding new category clearly intended to set them apart from his other works and, of course, from the works of all his competitors. Each print would boast "beauty and grandeur," and together they would constitute, promised the publisher, "a pictorial his-

tory of the Civil War as well as a gallery of magnificent art works."[41]

The inspiration, and sales pitch, for what the company confidently began promoting simply as "Prang's War Pictures" was decidedly patriotic. But the aspiration remained admirably artistic. The works were thoroughly researched and featured careful attention to such details as regimental flags, uniforms, and, of course, accurate portraits of its celebrated heroes. The artists took up correspondence with veterans to elicit details about specific incidents. Preliminary sketches were submitted in advance to those battle survivors "best qualified" to judge accuracy.[42]

Although designed to decorate the walls of loyal Union homes, the prints, all 17 x 23 inches in size, could alternatively be housed as a complete set in "an elegant portfolio of special design to hold the whole collection." This "easel portfolio," as Prang called it, was thus a precursor of today's conversation-piece, coffee-table books. A viewer examining the Prang portfolio would open the gold-stamped cover to reveal a box containing space to accommodate each print in "a maroon plush"

33

---

39. For an example of Thulstrup's work for the series, see *Charge of a Sutler Upon G. B. Anderson's Brigade at Gaines's Mill;* and for Davidson, see *The "Brooklyn" Attacked by the Confederate Ram "Tennessee,"* both in Robert Underwood Johnson and Clarence Clough Buel, eds., *Battles and Leaders of the Civil War* _ 4 vols. (New York: The Century Company, 1888):2:66, 358.

40. Holzer and Neely, *Union Image,* 95; Davidson was praised in the *Boston Daily Globe,* February 11, 1887, reprinted in Prang's 1888 *Prospectus,* 12.

41. *Prang War Pictures. Set of Twenty. . . .*

42. *Prang's War Pictures* (1888 Prospectus).

velvet mat. The title to each scene was subtly printed in soft lettering, not boldly proclaimed, as if to further remind prospective buyers of their claim to serious consideration as art.[43]

Most impressive of all, the prints all featured a rich but somber-hued color palette much unlike the unrelentingly bright chromos pouring off the presses of Kurz & Allison in Chicago. Prang wanted his pictures to look like oil paintings (though, ironically, all but one of them were based on watercolors, not oils[44]). So he imposed a sepia patina to the color mix that captured "the spirit of the originals" yet made the finished products resemble thickly varnished Old Masters. Against this muted background, splashes of red-white-and-blue on the flags, and light blue for the skies, stood out boldly. As the first prospectus for the series boasted, "The sparkle and brilliancy, combined with the most delicate graduations of light and shade, peculiar to water-color effects, are faithfully preserved." Prang had come a long way from the days in which he had given away free pencils to encourage buyers to apply colors of their own.[45]

The prospectus emphasized the attention Prang had paid to color. "Each picture," it boasted, "is a combination of over 300 colors and shades," adding, "Their superiority over black and white prints, in illustrating military scenes, is at once apparent, for the flags and the uniforms of the officers and troops are vividly reproduced, the fire and smoke of battle graphically portrayed, and all the surrounding represented in colors of nature and of actual war." The firm went so far as to claim that the prints were "the first illustrations, in color, ever issued in America on this subject"—though in reality, Kurz & Allison's Gettysburg chromo had preceded the Prang set by two full years.[46]

But Prang had no rival as a promoter. Wisely, he called on some of the surviving veterans of the battles to provide valuable endorsements that testified to the beauty and historical accuracy of his chromos. General John A. Logan, for example, one of the leaders of the Atlanta campaign, obliged by declaring, "The Prang War Pictures are marvellously well-executed, the color and drawings being true to nature." Admiral David Dixon Porter, a hero of the naval encounter at New Orleans, gave its depiction in chromo "my unqualified approbation,

43. Original in the Lincoln Museum, Fort Wayne, Indiana.

44. The originals are in the Seventh Regiment Fund collection, in the Seventh Regiment Armory in New York City. They are not yet accessible to the public. For reproductions of some, see Holzer and Neely, *Mine Eyes Have Seen the Glory.*

45. *Prospectus. Prang's War Pictures. Aquarelle Facsimile Prints* (Boston: L. Prang & Co., 1887), original in the Print Collection, Boston Public Library.

46. Ibid., and McClinton, *Chromolithographs of Louis Prang,* 147–48.

both as a work of art and as an accurate representation." General O. O. Howard, who had fought without much distinction at Gettysburg but later, with more success, supported William T. Sherman at Atlanta, stated, "Certainly the execution is admirable. . . . I think Prang's pictures generally are beginning to rival the best of paintings." And Sherman himself admired the chromo of Sheridan's charge at Winchester, hailing it as "a well executed picture accurately depicting the scene."[47]

There were more endorsements to come. General Alexander S. Webb, whose brigade was featured holding off Pickett's Charge in Prang's Gettysburg chromo, called that depiction "one of the best war pictures I have ever seen," adding, "It is as truthful a representation of what took place . . . as could be made." Even the elder statesman of American engraving, John Sartain of Philadelphia, was moved to respond to a request for his opinion by admitting, "Both the battles on land by de Thulstrup and those of Davidson of marine battles are so good that no one is likely to dispute their excellent artistic qualities. As to their reproduction as prints, it is enough to know that they are by Mr. Prang, of Boston, whose well-deserved reputation for faithful, intelligent, and spirited copies insures suc-

cess in that direction." As one wartime commander predicted of the prints: "They cannot fail to be highly prized, not only by comrades who participated in the scenes represented. . . ."[48]

Just to be sure, Prang hired a small army of his own—an army of veterans—to sell the pictures to old "comrades," as the agents called themselves and their prospective customers. One John V. Redpath was hired as the general agent on the project, and as Prang was busy heralding the artistic value of the series, agent Redpath and his salesmen emphasized the prints' historical reliability. Prospective customers were told that men like John A. Lynn, a hero of Kenesaw Mountain, for example, personally "made the final corrections in the artist's sketch" representing that battle.

It was surely no coincidence that Prang's hometown newspaper, the *Boston Daily Globe*, immediately recognized that the chromos were not "made in the haphazard manner of many so-called military pictures, but as the result of careful pain-taking, and the liberal expenditure of time and money. Battle-fields have been visited by the artists, access to official reports has been obtained, and war-time photographs in possession of the government have been secured." The "high degree of realism"

---

47. *Prang's War Pictures*, facsimile of undated prospectus in the author's collection; *Prang War Pictures. Set of Twenty. . . .*

48. Endorsements culled from the 1887 and 1888 Prang *Prospectus* pamphlets.

achieved by the Prang war pictures, the *Globe* noted, had been guaranteed when early sketches were submitted for review "to those best qualified to judge of the scenes represented"—in other words, veterans themselves. The result was "a triumph for American art" and a credit to the enterprising publisher.[49]

The *Boston Transcript* echoed these sentiments, praising the series as "exquisitely beautiful" and ". . . rendered in the highest style of art." And the *Philadelphia Sunday News* agreed that the results were "very remarkable works of art . . . beautiful enough to deserve a place in any gallery."[50]

The *Philadelphia Inquirer*'s art critic also lavished praised on what he called Prang's "new process of printing in watercolors." "It must be gratifying to the artists," he wrote the morning after Independence Day, 1886, "to see their works reproduced with so much of the spirit and character faithfully preserved, and it is an important step in the progress of culture and education that such really artistic works can be successfully brought within the reach of the great masses of the people. The new work is attracting a good deal of attention,

and it is only fair to say it repays critical examination."[51]

Prang's ambitious series would ultimately boast eighteen chromos: six depictions of eastern battles, six of western battles, and six of naval encounters, all issued to subscribers between 1886 and 1888. But the individual titles were released in no specific chronological order, apparently appearing as fast as they could be adapted and printed: a total of seven in 1886 (the Battle of Chattanooga, Sheridan's Charge at Winchester, Sheridan's Ride, Mobile Bay, the Siege of Vicksburg, the *Monitor* and *Merrimac* in "the first fight between ironclads," and the capture of New Orleans); nine in 1887 (Fredericksburg, Gettysburg, Spotsylvania, Kenesaw Mountain, the capture of Fort Fisher in North Carolina, the passing of the river batteries at Port Hudson, Louisiana, the duel between the *Kearsarge* and *Alabama* off Cherbourg, France, plus the battles of Antietam and Allatoona Pass); and two final chromos in 1888 (an artillery review at Atlanta and the Hornet's Nest at Shiloh).

The company even issued a bonus print (sent free to buyers once all the other prints were ordered and paid for): a Thulstrup *trompe l'oeil*–style chromo entitled *Grant from West Point to Appomattox* (fig. 16). It presented a handsome, central,

---

49. Ibid. Historian Mark E. Neely, Jr., found another copy of the *Boston Globe* article in the copy of the *Prospectus* at the Huntington Library's bound copy of the *Descriptive Texts* in San Marino, California. See Neely and Holzer, *Union Image*, 226–27, 251n.

50. *Prospectus* (1888).

---

51. *Philadelphia Inquirer* (July 5, 1886), reprinted in *Prospectus* (1887), 14.

FIG. 16.

L. Prang & Co., after Thure de Thulstrup, *Grant from West Point to Appomattox.* Boston, 1885. Chromolithograph, 23⁷/₈ x 17³/₄ inches. Probably issued as a mourning print for Grant, this large-format tribute featured a neat artistic trick: the central portrait was made to appear to be lying atop the smaller vignettes that highlighted Grant's life as a soldier. Clockwise from bottom left, the scenes showed Grant: graduating from West Point in 1843; fighting in Mexico at the Battle of Chapultepec in 1847; drilling Union volunteers in 1861; capturing Fort Donelson in 1862; supervising the long 1863 siege at Vicksburg; meeting Lincoln to receive his commission as lieutenant general in 1864; and accepting Lee's surrender at Appomattox in 1865. General William T. Sherman called this print "an ornament to any patriot's home, whether a log-cabin or a mansion on Fifth Avenue." Artist Thulstrup also pronounced the chromo reproduction "excellent," adding, "I don't think it could be excelled." (*Prospectus to Prang's War Pictures*) (*The Old Print Shop, New York*)

profile portrait of the Union's greatest hero surrounded by smaller depictions embellishing the border, representing the highlights of his military career, all "well-chosen and accurate as to uniform and details," as General Sherman testified.[52]

Grant was an obvious choice for such tributes, but the Prang firm's surviving records unfortunately shed little light on why other heroes and specific engagements were selected for the series, or why other choices were ignored. However, careful analysis of the portfolio yields some important clues about its commercial and political inspiration. Although painful Union battlefield defeats like Chancellorsville and the first and second Battles of Bull Run were understandably rejected to avoid exhuming bitter memories, Prang made every effort to produce chromos that would appeal to print-buying veterans of all branches of the military and all theaters of the war. Included were scenes of twelve land battles, five naval engagements, and one naval-marine assault. Five of the prints depicted engagements in Virginia, three in Georgia, two each in Louisiana and Tennessee, and one each in Pennsylvania, Maryland, Mississippi, Alabama, and North Carolina. Yet another print portrayed a fabled naval

duel off the coast of France. There would be something for everyone.

The chromos also reveal a bias toward successful, beloved generals, especially those who were still alive (or only recently deceased) and had remained popular and politically correct since the war. Understandably, neither Ambrose E. Burnside, who led the Army of the Potomac to inglorious disaster at Fredericksburg in 1862, nor Joseph Hooker, who was annihilated at Chancellorsville the following year, were portrayed in the Prang chromos. But neither was George Gordon Meade, who may have commanded the Union to victory at Gettysburg but who had died in 1872, fourteen long years before the prints began appearing. Prang perhaps concluded that Meade's appeal had waned.

On the other hand, Ulysses S. Grant, reverentially depicted in one particularly fine "war picture" and honored with portrayal in the bonus chromo as well, had served two terms as president of the United States and had died a hero's death only one year before Prang began publishing his war pictures. Moreover, Grant had written a wildly successful, posthumously published memoir, reinvigorating his popularity.

William T. Sherman, who dominated Prang's Battle of Atlanta chromo, had become general-in-chief of the army

---

52. The original Thulstrup watercolor is in the Anne S. K. Brown Military Collection, John Hay Library, Brown University.

after the war, won nearly as much acclaim fighting American Indians as he did fighting Confederates, and published his memoirs in 1875. He had retired from the service as recently as 1883, still greatly admired in the North. As for Philip H. Sheridan, the hero of not one but two of Prang's chromos, he also remained very much alive, having retired only one year earlier as Sherman's successor as general-in-chief. Now he was hard at work on an autobiography of his own. Louis Prang clearly preferred living heroes to dead ones.

Politics probably played a key role in his print choices as well. George B. McClellan may have won the Battle of Antietam, but his portrait did not grace the chromo representing that victory. One explanation for the slight may be that in 1864 McClellan had run for president against the sainted Lincoln, on a party platform that opposed the war. True, he later made a political comeback, serving as governor of New Jersey from 1878 to 1881. But although McClellan had died as recently as 1885, he had remained an unreconstructed Democrat, which may help account for his exclusion from Prang's war pictures. The only luminary who overcame the "handicap" of Democratic Party affiliation was Winfield Scott Hancock, who had narrowly lost the White House to James A. Garfield in 1880. Hancock, too, had run on the Democratic line. But Garfield, his assassination notwithstanding, was no Lincoln, and besides, Hancock had lived and remained prominent until February, 1886. The reverential obituaries that his death inspired doubtless moved Prang to allow him the central place in the series' Kenesaw Mountain chromo the following year, politics notwithstanding. "Hancock the Magnificent" was the one major exception to Prang's seeming Republicans-only rule.

More typical was the case of Republican General John A. "Black Jack" Logan. He had been a politician before the Civil War and resumed his career after peace was restored. Elected to the U.S. Senate in 1871, he sought the vice presidency in 1884 as James G. Blaine's running mate in what proved to be the first White House contest that the Republican Party lost since the days of Lincoln. But few blamed Logan. Moreover, the old general died just before the Prang series made its debut. And not long before, he had made certain, some whispered, that he would be heroically depicted in the Battle of Atlanta Cyclorama painted the same year that Prang set to work on his chromo series. Logan was one subject who knew the value of sympathetic depiction in art, so it was almost poetic justice that Prang would include him in his war pictures.

39

Judged solely as a political enterprise, Prang's portfolio would have to be counted a success. In 1888, after the last of the prints had appeared, the Republicans recaptured the White House, albeit without winning the popular vote. It was probably not lost on Prang's many patriotic customers that the new president, Benjamin Harrison, was, like most of them, a Union veteran of the Civil War.

Of course, Prang made certain that his political bias was ennobled by high artistic standards. An extraordinary degree of care was required to produce the chromos, and the publisher spared neither expense nor time to get the products right, hinting in his promotional brochures at a "new and secret process." The earlier, tinted battle prints by Currier & Ives of New York, and E. B. & E. C. Kellogg of Hartford, had been printed in black-and-white and then colored by hand. The process called for assembly lines of laborers applying, respectively, blues, greens, and reds. If one or another colorist accidentally slopped paint outside the margins of the outline drawing, it did not much matter. But Prang's chromos were *printed* in colors, meaning that each sheet went through the press several times, required precise register, and left no room for error. They *had* no outlines because Prang wanted them to look like paintings, not prints. Eight months were required just for drawing the watercolors on stone.

An early edition of *Prang's Chromo* provided detailed insight into the demanding process. Lithographic stones could only be of "a species of limestone found in Bavaria . . . wrought into thick slabs with finely polished surface." Each drawing was made directly on the stone "with a sort of colored soap, which adheres to the stone and enters into a chemical combination with the application of certain acids and gums." Then the stone was dampened with a sponge, and oil color applied with a printer's roller. "The drawing itself, being oily, repels the water, but retains the color applied."

Only heavy "'plate paper,' of the best quality" could be used; each sheet had to be durable enough to pass through the presses repeatedly, once for each application of color. The paper had to be precisely "registered"—described as "that part of a pressman's work which consists in so arranging the paper in the press, that it shall receive the impression on exactly the same spot of every sheet." The process was "repeated again and again and again; occasionally, as often as thirty times," after which the picture might still look more like "a spoiled colored photograph than . . . the charming picture that it eventually became." Only after all the colors had been successfully applied, and inspected, were finished prints dried, embossed, and varnished. Such work required highly trained specialists:

> The process thus briefly explained, we need hardly add, requires equally great skill and judgment at every stage. A single error is instantly detected by the practised [*sic*] eye in the finished specimen. The production of a chromo, if it is at all complicated, requires several months—sometimes several years—of careful preparation. The mere drawing of the different and entirely-detached parts on so many different stones is of itself a work that requires an amount of labor and a degree of skill, which, to a person unfamiliar with the process, would appear incredible.

No less exhaustive was the formidable marketing effort Prang launched on behalf of his Civil War series. In Philadelphia, his agents staged a private viewing of the first proofs in June, 1886, for both "distinguished military men" and journalists, then solicited their favorable comments in writing. A pleased representative of the *Philadelphia Sunday News* happily reported on the afternoon reception at the rooms of agents Faulkner and Allan and obligingly lauded the "rich, vivid, and natural" quality of the chromos on display there. "Art connoisseurs and representatives of the press" were similarly summoned to a showing in Washington, D.C. The letters of praise these preview exhibitions invariably inspired were then proudly featured in Prang's advertising materials. Surviving sales records are sketchy, but every indication points to their robust and enduring popularity among print buyers and, later, with collectors.[53]

Original subscribers would receive their pictures in deliveries of two each, "in stout paper covers." First offered at $20 for each set of six, or $60 for the complete set, the price to subscribers was discounted at some point to "$5 for each set of two, or $45 the set."

The first "part" would bring chromos of *Sheridan's Final Charge at Winchester*, promoted as "a most spirited picture of the dashing cavalry charge," and *The Monitor and Merrimac: The First Fight Between Ironclads*, "most accurate in its details, and impressive in its composition and its action." The next installment would include *Battle of Chattanooga, November 25, 1863*, a scene "of fierce grandeur, and at the time depicted, one

41

---

53. *Prospectus* (1887).

of intense anxiety and suspense, for every hero in that human wave surging up the mountain-side realized that it must be victory or death"; and *Capture of New Orleans*, "a brilliant representation of that famous battle by night, showing the Mississippi squadron, under Commodore Farragut, passing Forts Philip and Jackson. . . ."[54]

Finally, the third set would consist of *Sheridan's Ride to the Battle of Cedar Creek, Oct. 19, 1864*, a "dashing scene" of the "famous episode of the war"; and *Battle of Fredericksburg: Laying Ponton Bridges under Fire*, another "spirited picture" of "one of the most important divisions of the service connected with the movement of armies." Future war pictures, the prospectus promised, would depict "scenes from other memorable battles, both on land and water." Prang concluded this early advertisement by stressing the firm's confident belief that the company was "so well known, to all interested in art publications, that a simple assurance, on their part, of conscientious painstaking in carrying out the details of this work will be regarded as a sufficient guarantee of good faith, and of excellence of execution."[55]

L. Prang & Co. eventually grouped the eighteen "war pictures" into three sets of six chromos each: eastern land battles, western land battles, and naval battles. Thereafter they were consistently packaged and repackaged under these categories, regardless of original publication date or subsequent price discounting.

It is impossible to know how many sets of the Prang prints were sold at any price, but the series did remain in Prang's catalogues for the rest of the century, offered at various discounts over the years. By 1900, one advertisement promised, the "splendid gallery of Art" had become available to be "placed in your home for only $2.00 and then 6 cents a day in payments," or only $20 for all sixteen, along with not one, but two, bonus prints: the Thulstrup portrait of Grant and a chromo of the *Naval Battle of Manila Bay*. Yet another war had come and gone, but Prang's Civil War chromos remained on the market.[56]

Surely, one of the secrets to their longtime success was the lavish way they were packaged, and one of the key elements of that packaging was their so-called "Descriptive Texts." As the very first prospectus for the chromos promised, "Each will be

---

54. *Prospectus. Prang's War Pictures.* Facsimile of original at the Prang-Mark Society, Watkins Glen, New York. (Boston: L. Prang & Co., 1888).

55. Ibid.

56. *Prang's War Pictures. Set of Twenty. . . .*

accompanied by a description, in letter press, written by an authority on the special incident it represents. These descriptions will be printed on excellent paper, in pamphlet form, octavo size, making a volume that will be a valuable work of reference." Eventually, the texts came to 188 pages that—though never published since—provide not only a "valuable work of reference" to the crucial land and sea battles of the Civil War but also rare insight into the way visual and historical memory was preserved for Americans in the last quarter of the nineteenth century.[57]

As for Prang, he thrived through the 1890s, growing wealthy and winning medals for his lifetime of accomplishments in picture publishing. He successfully launched a Prang Education Co. in 1882 and then merged with the Taber Art Company of New Bedford in 1892, moving the new firm to Springfield, Massachusetts, and specializing in chromos of Old Master paintings. But his credentials as a patron of living artists was unsurpassed. When he finally retired in 1898, widely acknowledged as the dean of American printmakers and the industry's most brilliant promoter, Prang liquidated his stock by selling the firm's original works of commissioned art at auction. More than 440 went on the block. Another sale seven years later offered 1,515 more originals. Such had been the extent of the lithographer's generosity with American painters.[58]

Some years earlier, on the occasion of the twenty-fifth anniversary of the founding of L. Prang & Co., one of the firm's resident greeting-card verse-writers, Miss E. S. Forman, had penned a poetic tribute to the publishing veteran. "In Honorem Louis Prang," as she called it, acknowledged the printmaker's special contributions to the national memory of its bloodiest conflict:

> *To War's red victor, wreaths and praise*
> *We fling, and tell his deeds in song;*
> *But Art deserves our greenest bays,*
> *Our sweetest notes to her belong.*
>
> *Honor to him, Art's steadfast friend,*
> *Who through the weary, waiting years,*
> *Has kept his faith, foreseen the end,*
> *His soul unswerved by hopes or fears;*

**43**

---

57. *Prospectus* (1888).

58. Pierce and Slautterback, *Boston Lithography*, 149; Marzio, *Democratic Art*, 94–95. The Prang-Taber firm stayed in business until 1937.

*Who ne'er has lost his lofty aim,*
*Nor ever stooped for sordid pelf;*
*But lived unheeding praise or blame,*
*True to his art and to himself.*[59]

44 Audiences remained true as well. Prang's Civil War prints long outlived their publisher, who died in California in 1909. Five titles went on to be reprinted in Benson Lossing's influential 1912 book, *History of the Civil War.* And throughout the twentieth century, Prang's works were eagerly collected and catalogued by both public institutions and private aficionados. A catalogue for Goodspeed's Book Shop in 1961 judged the Civil War series as "a triumph" that "may be considered his finest production in the field of pictorial Americana & also the handsomest Civil War prints ever made." The writer noted that "their mellow coloring, in quality so much like that of original oil paintings, is in pleasing contrast to the more gar-

ish War prints extant. . . ." The individual pictures could be had then for only $35 apiece. But at a sale at Christie's in 1999, their value had risen sharply to between $2,000 and $3,000 each.[60]

The general public's taste for most nineteenth-century American popular prints long ago yielded to those technological advances that made it possible for pictures to move and, later, to talk. Modern Americans get their images from television and the worldwide web, and few of us still hang patriotic Civil War pictures on our living room walls. Those who do seem to favor contemporary work by artists like Mort Künstler, Keith Rocco, and Don Troiani.

But in his day, it was Louis Prang who vividly brought art, color, and history into American homes. Thirty years after the guns had stilled, and for generations after, Prang gave to the war's survivors, and their descendants, a way to recall the Civil War with pride. His prints still evoke the drama and glory of that convulsive national nightmare.

59. "E.S.F.," *In Honorem Louis Prang,* from the L. Prang & Co. silver anniversary album, *The Prang Souvenir,* original copy in the Doris Jeffrey Collection, Mount Kisco, New York, reprinted in Jeffrey, "Happy Birthday, Louis Prang!", *The Antique Trader Weekly* (March 14, 1979):79.

60. Goodspeed's Book Shop, Boston, Catalogue *At Goodspeed's* (April 1961): 213–15; Christie's East, *Fine Antique Firearms, Swords, and Civil War Memorabilia* (New York: May 11, 1999):17.

# A NOTE ON THE "TEXTS" TO
## *Prang's War Pictures*

Each [print] will be accompanied by a description, in letter press, written by an authority on the special incident it represents. These descriptions will be printed on excellent paper, in pamphlet form, octavo size, so as to enable the subscriber to bind his whole collection in one volume for permanent preservation.

—Undated ca. 1886 advance advertisement for *Prang's War Pictures*

L. Prang & Co. issued the so-called "texts" to its series of Civil War pictures as eighteen separately printed brochures, one text for each of the prints. To Americans of the late 1880s, they must have seemed nearly as ambitious as the pictures themselves. Each 5 x 8–inch pamphlet arrived with its own distinctive, salmon-colored cover, and each offered a succinct, authoritative history of a Civil War battle, punctuated with firsthand recollections by well-known eyewitnesses to the specific action depicted in the corresponding chromo.

They also featured rare insights into the artistic inspiration for each scene: clues to help print buyers understand precisely why military painter Thure de Thulstrup, for example, chose to highlight a certain moment of a land battle, or how marine artist Julian O. Davidson selected a naval encounter. Some *Texts* also provided maps, as well as detailed keys to the more complicated scenes, reliably identifying the characters and accessories portrayed. In short, the *Texts* were appealing, original, and, in some cases, indispensable.

Nothing as ambitious as these *Texts* had ever before been offered to the public to accompany popular prints. The picture-publishing industry was still learning how best to sell itself in the mid-1880s. Until then, its marketing efforts had largely been limited to simple catalogues, sporadic newspaper advertising, and the occasional pamphlet, although Louis Prang was always in the vanguard, publishing his own newsletter for a time when he could not generate enough publicity in the newspapers. Even so, his *Texts* represented an all but revolutionary approach to promoting prints both aggressively and seriously. Their appearance placed potential buyers on notice that Prang's Civil War chromos were, at their most obvious level, worthy of unprecedented narrative accompaniment and, second, had been exhaustively researched and thoughtfully conceived. These were not carelessly imagined pictures, like the hackneyed prints that had poured off the presses to satisfy audience thirst for battle pictures while the war raged. Here was pictorial history equal to narrative history—and vice versa.

If nothing else, the *Texts* were formidable: 64 pages devoted to the company's six prints of eastern land battles, another 66 pages devoted to western land battles, and 58 more devoted to naval battles—188 pages of written material altogether, a staggering total when one remembers that the brochures were issued principally as promotional tools, not as history. To print buyers of the day, the sheer volume of these written accompaniments must have seemed just as compelling as, a century later, the book-of-the-month-style Time-Life Civil War series would become to their own loyal subscribers. Until the Prang project, never before had mass-produced Civil War pictures been supplemented by such detailed written explanation. Taken as a whole—and several of the surviving copies were later bound together by avid collectors who clearly regarded them as a worthy package—the material constitutes nothing less than a concise history of the major actions of the war, as seen through the unique prism of both its participants and its portrayers.

But why recall and republish them more than a century after they first appeared? Surely, other, more detailed battle histories were written both before and after Prang's *Texts*. True enough, but it is also safe to say that no other war history ever illuminated the process by which artists analyzed battles, searching for that one inspirational moment worthy of depiction. No other text ever attempted to explain why such selections were made, and none detailed precisely what had occurred at the exact moment being portrayed. Certainly, none made so ambitious and sober an appeal to print buyers. For modern readers, the *Texts* provide reliable war history and unprecedented iconographical history alike. Besides, its eyewitness recollections remain eminently readable.

Perhaps most important of all, the *Texts* shed new light onto the public taste and collective memory of the first postwar generation—war veterans and their descendants as well as the widows and orphans of its casualties—through their patronage of one of the most ambitious and influential Civil War picture-publishing projects of the nineteenth century. How this generation chose to recall the conflict would influence American attitudes for the next century, as the reunited nation strove to heal its wounds without abandoning its memories.

Until now, historians have looked primarily to written sources for evidence of these yearnings; but in recent years, it has become increasingly clear that public memory was also informed by images. Memory was influenced by statuary that was built to be displayed in public places, as well as by prints, like Prang's, designed to decorate private places, like the walls of the cherished family parlor. People who purchased these prints and subscribed to these texts were testifying to unwaver-

ing patriotism and a resolute conviction that the war had been worth the sacrifice. They firmly believed that its brave heroes and technological miracles were worth recalling and honoring.

Finally, for modern aficionados and collectors who have been as charmed by Prang's luminous Civil War chromos as were their original audiences more than a century ago, the *Texts*, since then largely unknown and all but unavailable, open windows onto the long-elusive mystery of why the firm chose such unusual battlefield perspectives for its series.

We still do not know the identity of the writer or writers who produced these *Texts* (only that they were done by noted "authorities" on the battles; Prang preferred omniscient authority to individual credit). But their efforts liberally incorporated the historic and artistic sensibilities informing painters Thulstrup and Davidson. In these *Texts* can be found not only *what* Prang published but, in some cases, *why*.

At the very least, what Prang said of the texts then can as convincingly be stated now. They remain "a valuable work of reference" on the Civil War and how we remember it. And, inarguably, they have been ignored for far too long.

For this, the first republication of the *Texts* to *Prang's War Pictures*, the written material is presented almost exactly as it first

47

appeared in its original form from 1886 to 1888, with one major exception.

The initial installment of the series actually appeared under the title *Text to First Part of Prang's War Pictures* and offered written material to accompany not one but two prints: *Sheridan's Final Charge at Winchester* and *Monitor and Merrimac.* Later, Prang would issue but one *Text* per chromo, seldom combining two titles in a single brochure. The exception is easy enough to explain. The firm undoubtedly debuted its series by publishing the *Sheridan* and the *Monitor and Merrimac* chromos first, and as a pair—both bear an 1886 copyright date—to demonstrate that the rest of the forthcoming series would boast the breadth to portray both land and sea battles accurately and beautifully.

Later on in the series of *Texts,* when the time came to issue brochures about additional naval engagements, the firm republished its *Monitor and Merrimac* brochure in sequence, as the fourteenth in its eighteen-pamphlet series. For the purposes of this republication, the material is included only once—as number fourteen, in its ultimate position within the final grouping of naval battle pictures. Aside from this modification to avoid repetition, little else has been altered.

As a result, the material includes occasional editorial and punctuation inconsistencies that were inevitable in a publishing series that appeared over a two-year period and represented the work of several writers and memoirists. The overabundance of commas, the countless ellipses and inset quotes that ran with superfluous quotation marks, have all been retained in the interest of presenting the series as it originally appeared. The occasional misspelled name has been noted, but the use of the editorial imposition "*sic*" has been stringently limited to preserve the flavor and flow of the original as closely as possible.

L. Prang & Co. was not particularly careful about making consistent the titles it assigned to each of its chromos. More often than not, the caption of an individual print did not match the title appearing on the cardboard cover for the corresponding *Text,* especially in proof editions of the chromos (which bore no title at all) or later editions (which sometimes carried new titles). Moreover, the first page of each *Text* usually bore a title different from that on the cover. To simplify matters, each text reproduced here bears only the title found on its initial page. The color-plate section of this book presents the "official" titles found on the prints themselves, as well as the alternate, "promotional" titles featured in the firm's publicity materials, brochures, advertisements, and the salmon-colored *Text* covers.

Finally, as a service to modern readers, the editor has provided the given names (in brackets) for each first mention of the more than one hundred Union and Confederate generals who were originally identified in the *Texts* to *Prang's War Pictures* by family name only.

Otherwise, the *Texts* required no editing, and in order to offer a faithful republication, none has been imposed.

As the *Texts* contend at one point, "neither generals nor their commanders were schooled in the art of war" before the appearance of Prang's chromos. These prints, together with their long-ignored narrative accompaniment, helped introduce "the art of war" not only to the participants, but to their descendants, and posterity.

# SHERIDAN'S
## *Final Charge* AT *Winchester*

On the 19th of September, 1864, on the line of the Opequan Creek, near Winchester, Va., in the Shenan doah Valley, this fight between the Union forces under General Philip H. Sheridan and the Confederates under General Jubal Early took place.

It resulted in the total defeat of Early, and was the first of a series of important contests between the same commanders for the control of the valley, which terminated in its ultimate evacuation by the Southern army.

A peculiarity of this engagement was the boldness and versatility with which the Union cavalry were handled. In no other battle of the war was the field better adapted for the operations of cavalry, on foot or mounted, and in none other was there more use of the sabre made than on this occasion.

Sheridan's mounted force numbered about six thousand men under General [Alfred T. A.] Torbert, and was distributed in three divisions, under Generals [Wesley] Merritt, [James H.] Wilson, and [William W.] Averell respectively.

In Merritt's First Division there were three brigades, and it is an incident in the service of one of these—known as the Cavalry Reserve Brigade (also as the "Regular" Brigade)—that is the subject of the picture. The Regular Brigade was commanded by Colonel Charles R. Lowell (a nephew of the late Minister to England), who was killed at the head of his command Oct 18, 1864. It consisted of the First, Second, and Fifth United States regiments of cavalry, Second Massachusetts and First New York Dragoons.

General Sheridan's line was formed with his infantry (parts of the Sixth, Eighth, and Nineteenth Corps) in the centre, Wilson's cavalry division on the left, while Merritt and Averell on the right wheeled gradually to the left and south, pivoting on the infantry, and seeking to envelop the enemy's left and rear.

The moment chosen by the artist was when the Union cavalry had nearly accomplished the last-named purpose, near the close of the day and of the battle, which lasted from 2 A.M. until 6 P.M.

The final and decisive movement of the cavalry, of which the charge of the Regular Brigade was part, is thus referred to in the official reports.

General Sheridan says: "I returned to the right, where the enemy was still fighting, with obstinacy, in the open ground in front of Winchester, and ordered Torbert to collect his cavalry and charge."

General Early states: "The enemy's cavalry again charged around my left flank, and the men began to give way again."

General Merritt reports: "Soon Colonel Lowell (Reserve Brigade) entered the lists. His heroic brigade—now reduced to about six hundred men—rode out fearlessly within five hundred yards of the enemy's line of battle, on the left of which, resting on an old earthwork, was a two-gun battery. The order was given to charge the line and get the guns."

Lieutenant Harrison, of the Second United States Cavalry, which was the leading regiment in Lowell's column in the charge referred to, writes as follows: "It was well toward four o'clock, and though the sun was warm the air was cool and bracing. The ground to our front was open and level, in some places, as a well-cut lawn. Not an obstacle intervened between us and the enemy's line, which was seen nervously awaiting our attack. The brigade was in column of squadrons, the Second United States Cavalry in front. At the sound of the bugle we took the trot, the gallop, and then 'the charge.' As we neared their line, we were welcomed by a fearful musketry fire, which temporarily confused the leading squadron, and caused the entire brigade to oblique slightly to the right. Instantly officers cried out, 'Forward!' 'Forward!' The men raised their sabres, and responded with deafening cheers. Within a hundred yards of the enemy's line we struck a blind ditch, but crossed it without breaking our front. In a moment we were face to face with the enemy. They stood for an instant, and then broke in complete rout. In this charge the battery and many prisoners were captured. Our own loss was severe, and of the officers of the Second, Captain Rodenbough (commanding the regiment) lost an arm, and Lieutenant Harrison was taken prisoner."[1]

The writer of this brief sketch of the circumstances attending the charge of Lowell's Brigade was among the group of officers at the head of the column, as shown in the picture, and distinctly remembers certain details which M. de Thulstrup has reproduced with rare fidelity.

The Union brigade colors, carried behind Colonel Lowell, are faithfully copied from the original flag, now in the Museum at West Point, and the artist has faithfully portrayed the atmospheric tone of an autumn day in Virginia, particularly of the day and hour in question.

At the time of the volley of musketry referred to by Lieutenant Harrison, the writer spoke to General Custer (represented in black sombrero and red cravat, on right flank of leading squadron), who assisted to encourage the men, and rode along with us for some distance. The officer on the white horse is an excellent representation of Lowell, the brigade commander. On his left were two regimental commanders,

1. Harrison, "Everglade to Cañon." New York: D. Van Nostrand.

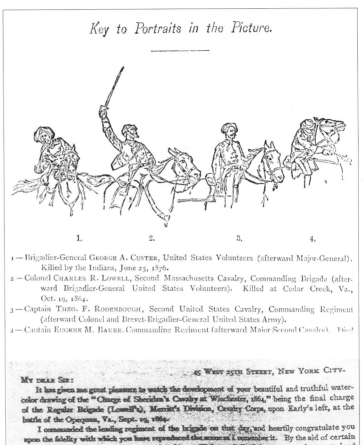

Key to Portraits in the Picture.

1.      2.      3.      4.

1 — Brigadier-General GEORGE A. CUSTER, United States Volunteers (afterward Major-General). Killed by the Indians, June 25, 1876.
2 — Colonel CHARLES R. LOWELL, Second Massachusetts Cavalry, Commanding Brigade (afterward Brigadier-General United States Volunteers). Killed at Cedar Creek, Va., Oct. 19, 1864.
3 — Captain THEO. F. RODENBOUGH, Second United States Cavalry, Commanding Regiment (afterward Colonel and Brevet-Brigadier-General United States Army).
4 — Captain EUGENE M. BAKER, Commanding Regiment (afterward Major Second Cavalry). Died

45 WEST 25TH STREET, NEW YORK CITY.
MY DEAR SIR:
It has given me great pleasure to watch the development of your beautiful and truthful water-color drawing of the "Charge of Sheridan's Cavalry at Winchester, 1864," being the final charge of the Regular Brigade (Lowell's), Merritt's Division, Cavalry Corps, upon Early's left, at the battle of the Opequan, Va., Sept. 19, 1864.
I commanded the leading regiment of the brigade on that day, and heartily congratulate you upon the fidelity with which you have reproduced the scene as I remember it. By the aid of certain soldiers who saw the charge from opposite sides, — Union and Confederate, — you have attained an exceptional degree of realism in the composition of your picture.
Very truly yours,
THEO. F. RODENBOUGH,
Bt.-Brig.-Gen. U.S.A.
TO MR. THURE DE THULSTRUP.

55

Captain Rodenbough of the Second and Captain Baker of the First Cavalry; also Captain Smith and Lieutenant Harrison of the Second Cavalry; and others whose positions are not remembered.

The Confederate standard-bearer had ventured too far from his escort, and when first seen by the writer was just in rear of the enemy's skirmish-line, urging his horse at full speed in a vain effort to rejoin his friends.

The Confederate guns—one of which is seen in the foreground—are understood to have belonged to "Lee's Battery." Before the brigade reached the point indicated in the picture, a number of men and horses had gone down under the spasmodic fire of the enemy.

One officer, severely wounded, was lying on the ground in the wake of the charging "Yankee" horsemen, when a handsome "Rebel" cavalier, well-mounted and clad in exceptionally bright gray uniform, rode up. The last comer was evidently trying to rejoin his command, which had changed its base since he left it. With a quick look around he saw the coast, for the moment, was clear. Dismounting he approached the fallen foe, and, after a courteous inquiry as to the extent of his injury, he proceeded to confiscate such contraband of war as a pistol and a pair of small field-glasses, bearing on the rims, in gilt letters, the owner's name. As he remounted he said to the Union officer, with a frank and graceful air, "I am sorry to leave you, but your own people will soon find you; while you are up we will fight you, but when down would care for you. But this is no place for me," he added, and with a wave of the hand this knight of the nineteenth century disappeared as suddenly as he had arrived.

To some of their prisoners the Confederates expressed the greatest admiration of the final charge of Sheridan's cavalry (part of which is here faithfully depicted), which was the finishing stroke to the operations of the day which sent the routed army of General Early "whirling through Winchester."

56

# LAYING THE PONTONS AT
## *Fredericksburg*

It is the night of the 10th of December, 1862 on the banks of that famous Virginian river which flows silently near the birthplace of Washington. A thick fog has settled down upon the town of Fredericksburg and vicinity. Winter has come, and, under the axe of "Yank" and "Reb" alike, the forests have melted and the hillsides are almost bare of trees.

Could we brush away the mist for a moment, we would see innumerable huts, surmounted by canvas, with countless camp-fires to show where the hosts of Lee and Burnside, like wild beasts preparing to spring, confront each other. The Rappahannock, filled with broken ice, runs with a swift current between the armies, as if in mute protest at the strife which seems inevitable.

On the left bank all appears as usual—an army sleeping; yet at midnight a Confederate spy may note signs of a move at the headquarters of the engineers, and erelong, with a low rumble, the ponton trains pull out of their park, and in several strings move toward the river.

But the wagons cannot go to the water's edge, and the heavy bridge material is carried thither by willing hands and on brawny shoulders. There are six bridges to be laid: two at "the Rope Ferry," just above the centre of the town; one opposite the lower end; and three, side by side, about a mile below

Fredericksburg. It is important to complete the work under cover of the darkness and of the fog. Can this be done?

On the opposite side the pickets are wide awake. For some days a movement of the Army of the Potomac has been expected. General [William] Barksdale, commanding the brigade whose duty it is to guard the Confederate front, has two able subordinates in Lieutenant-Colonel Fizer, of the 17th, and Lieutenant-Colonel Luse, of the 18th Mississippi Infantry. To the first named he has confided the line from a point just above the town to one just below, where Luse's regiment continues the protection of the river front to the mouth of Deep Creek, a small stream emptying into the river a mile south of Fredericksburg.

The entire force thus guarding the river consists of the 8th Florida, 13th, 17th, 21st, and 18th Mississippi Regiments, in the order named from left to right,—later to be re-enforced by the 15th South Carolinians and 16th Georgians.

It is now two o'clock on the morning of the 11th. The fog seems to thicken, and the Southern videttes frequently pause and peer anxiously into the gloom, depending more upon ear than eye for the first sign of danger. One tall Mississippian gets down on all-fours until his cheek is near the earth; he has detected the rumble of wheels, and then a regular dropping sound, as when boards are laid one on top of each other; he

calls the corporal of his reserve, and soon the bustle on the opposite shore becomes more distinct: is the enemy preparing to cross? Similar sounds are reported farther down the river.

The commander of the Confederate pickets reports his discovery to the division commander, and is admonished to be ready to oppose the crossing.

At 3 A.M. the first ponton is anchored on the left or Union bank of the stream, and work is pushed forward with alacrity on all the bridges at once. To four of these structures General [Daniel P.] Woodbury, of the Engineers, gives his personal attention; the workmen being under the immediate direction of Major Spaulding, 50th New York Infantry, at the upper three (or town) bridges, and Major Magruder, 15th New York Infantry, at two lower ones; Lieutenant Cross, U.S.A., having charge of the Sixth Bridge, which is laid rapidly and almost silently by the trained and disciplined battalion of regular "Sappers and Miners." The gallant 7th Michigan and 19th Massachusetts Infantry are deployed along the river bank as skirmishers to cover the pontoniers.

It is no child's play, this ponton-bridge building. To creep upon the enemy's position, breech-loader in hand, under cover of a fog, rapidly, silently, hoping to surprise him, or to meet him on somewhat equal terms, is one thing. It is another to construct a bridge laboriously *toward* the enemy, under cover

58

of a cloud, which, while it conceals his position, does not muffle the sound of your mallet or of each plank as it drops into its place, and brings you closer to the other shore, where some one is waiting to welcome you to a hospitable grave. This was, doubtless, in the minds of some of the bridge-builders as they worked cautiously out into the stream.

Five o'clock in the morning has come. The fog has lifted slightly; the Rappahannock sweeps sullenly under the new obstructions to its free passage; the bridges loom out upon the sight of the waiting sentinels on the right bank; the pontoniers work more slowly, despite the encouraging words of their officers, albeit the work is two thirds accomplished.

Suddenly from the heights directly opposite the line of bridges comes the loud report of two cannon. It is the signal to the Army of Northern Virginia that their old enemy, the Army of the Potomac, is about to make a morning call, and must have a warm reception. Immediately from the picket line there dart flashes of flame and the sharp reports of small arms; men are seen to drop here and there on the bridges, and a rush is made for the Union side and cover. Captain Perkins, a gallant officer of the 50th New York, and two other officers and a number of men are wounded. And now the right centre division of General [Henry J.] Hunt's corps of artillery pours upon the assailants shot and shell, until every living thing on the other side seeks shelter from the iron storm which threatens to destroy the historic town and leave "not one stone upon another." But as suddenly as it commenced, the storm subsides.

What next? The bridges must be laid. Time is precious. An army is waiting!

The lower bridges are not molested until 8:15 A.M., when a volley from Luse's command wounds five men and temporarily suspends operations; but the Confederates, at this point being without much shelter, are speedily dispersed by the Union artillery, and these bridges are completed soon after nine o'clock.

In the mean while General Woodbury has been arranging for another effort to complete the town bridges. At 10 A.M. he leads eighty volunteers from the 8th Connecticut Infantry to the upper bridge, and with one half of the detachment as a support, the other half essays to work. These fare no better than their predecessors. A volley from the Mississippians disperses them. Woodbury is in despair. As he afterward reported, "I was greatly mortified in the morning to find that the pontoniers under my command would not continue at work until actually shot down. The officers and some of the men showed a willingness to do so, but the majority seemed to think their task a hopeless one." The General adds, "*Perhaps I was unreasonable!*"

As the result of several conferences between Generals Hunt and Woodbury, and Colonel Hall, commanding the advanced brigade of the Army of the Potomac, it was arranged that the 7th Michigan and 19th Massachusetts shall cross the river in boats, and, in the face of the enemy, occupy the ground at the water's edge, while the bridge-builders push forward their work.

The defence of the town is in able and gallant hands. The low buildings of honest old-time masonry, and the cellars of the other houses, and the loopholed block-house near the railroad bridge, are filled with sharpshooters and their reserves.

At 3 P.M., Lieutenant-Colonel Baxter, with seventy-five men of the 7th Michigan, enter six pontons and push gallantly across under a sharp fire, and not without loss; one man is killed, and the detachment commander and several men are wounded.[1] As the boats touch the bank, the party dash forward upon the first street, carry the position, and capture thirty-one prisoners, with a loss of one officer and one man killed and several wounded. The remainder of the regiment has by this time crossed, together with the 19th Massachusetts, which is placed on the right of the brigade line.

Immediately after this operation, or in connection with it, one hundred men from the 89th New York Volunteers, under

Captain Hazley, cross in the same way at the lower town bridge, and capture sixty-four prisoners, including three small companies of the 8th Florida.

Thus the Army of the Potomac has secured a footing upon the Confederate side, but the bridges are not completed until some time after, and the safety of Colonel Hall's advance guard has been jeopardized. Indeed, the operations at Fredericksburg, from beginning to end, on the Union part, were marked by vacillation and absence of ordinary forethought, and were only redeemed by the grand spectacle of American heroism and endurance exhibited by the troops.

It is not necessary here to attempt a description of the operations which followed the construction of the bridges; how the two great masses of armed men, discarding on the one side the simplest rules of the art of war, and on the other availing themselves of the abundant natural and artificial aids at hand, battled brutally for the mastery; until, bruised and bleeding, but defiant still, the one retired to bind up its wounds and gather strength for another and triumphant encounter; the other encouraged to prolong the strife with a devotion and daring worthy of the best cause. As a grand illustration of American valor, the battle of Fredericksburg will rank with the great historic combats of mankind.

---

1. This is the operation shown in the picture.

# Sheridan's Ride

The most dramatic episode of the famous "Ride," which lights up the sombre pages of the history of the Great Rebellion, even as the "Charge of the Six Hundred" sparkles among the shadows of European warfare, has hitherto escaped the notice of artist and author. It has been reserved for M. de Thulstrup to mark this incident by the accompanying picture which might well be entitled "The Home Stretch."

To understand its full significance, a few words are proper in explanation.

On the night of the 17th of October, 1864, a train drew up to the platform of the Baltimore and Ohio Railroad station at Martinsburg, West Virginia, and a few passengers alighted. Some of them were convalescents returning to their regiments; four or five were evidently commissioned officers, although displaying but little sign of rank. One of these was almost hidden within the folds of a great-coat, and his features were concealed by a dark blue cloth hat pulled well down over his eyes. He was quite short, walked quickly, and was evidently "one in authority." The country thereabout was swarming with guerillas or "partisan troops," as they were mildly called by the Confederate government. Could [Colonel John Singleton] Mosby or [Captain Harry] Gilmor then have dreamed of the prize almost within their grasp, and of what moment, to

62

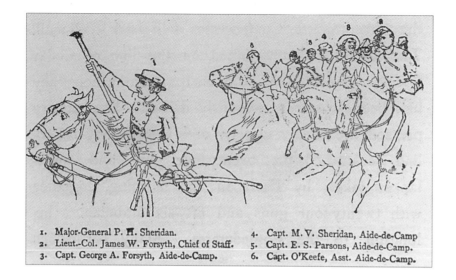

1. Major-General P. H. Sheridan.
2. Lieut.-Col. James W. Forsyth, Chief of Staff.
3. Capt. George A. Forsyth, Aide-de-Camp.
4. Capt. M. V. Sheridan, Aide-de-Camp
5. Capt. E. S. Parsons, Aide-de-Camp.
6. Capt. O'Keefe, Asst. Aide-de-Camp.

the Southern cause, the capture of that person meant, perhaps the "Ride" might have been indefinitely postponed, and the region re-christened with the name, once so familiar to Northern ears, of "the Valley of Humiliation."

Within the hospitable walls of the little inn, at this time and place, a young captain of regular cavalry, who had left an arm upon the plain in front of Winchester scarce one month before, was resting, preparatory to taking a train for his home. After the travellers had made sad havoc with the landlord's fare, the entire party visited the chamber of the convalescent.

It was nearly midnight. Between the sheets of a feather bed reclined the invalid, talking with a small but compactly built, bronzed, and pleasant-voiced man, who lounged carelessly on the counterpane, while his feet dangled far above the floor. Scattered about the room were others of the party, now arrayed in the uniform of their rank. The little man wore the stars of a major-general; the others, leaves or bars.

The Major-General was describing his plans for a grand

guerilla hunt which he proposed to have very soon. The cavalry were to be deployed as skirmishers in the Valley of the Shenandoah, then moved forward across country, over hill and dale, the line contracting as it advanced, beating up bushwhacker haunts, and finally, seine-like, enclosing the freebooters who infested that region. An hour passed thus; and having exhausted their pipes, the visitors withdrew, wishing the wounded man *bon voyage*. The writer will ever retain a pleasant memory of that visit from the hero of the "Ride."

The combination of circumstances that enabled [General Jubal] Early to steal upon the Union forces at Cedar Creek and strike them a severe blow; that aided the temporary commander of the Federals to check the Confederate advance; that brought to bear upon the situation at a critical moment the exceptional personal qualities of Sheridan,—whereby his broken regiments were re-formed, his lines strengthened, confidence restored, and an aggressive movement made which ended in the total rout of the enemy,—these are matters of history.

It is sufficient for the purpose of explaining the incident pictured by M. de Thulstrup, to say that it was the culmination of the grand gallop from Winchester, which began on the outskirts of that town when the sound of cannon and the echoes of musketry warned General Sheridan that something more than an affair of outposts was happening.

How the General put spurs to his noble black charger "Rienzi," with prompt response from the surprised animal, and as he swept along shouted words of encouragement to the fugitives who in swarms were making to the rear; how he dropped a staff officer here and there on the road to gather up and turn back the stragglers, of whom more than two thousand were brought back to their regiments by a single cavalry squadron; how the thoroughly aroused leader came upon the scene of the morning's discomfiture during a lull in the operations (caused partly by the temptation to plunder, which overcame Early's troops, and the stout resistance to his advance by the Union cavalry and the Sixth Corps); how he took in the features of the battle arena in an instant and prepared to assume the offensive,—have been themes of poetry and prose.

As we have already said, this was merely preliminary to the grand burst of speed which distanced Early, landed his opponent at the winning post, and brought "Sheridan's Ride" to a triumphant close.

"From the moment that he saw the situation of the battle, he had determined not to allow the enemy to remain in possession of the field, but to recover it as soon as all should be ready for attack. This assurance he gave to the troops as he rode along the lines, and the splendid inspiration of his presence was the best omen of coming victory."[1] At 4 P.M. Sheridan ordered an advance, and the whole Union line gallantly responded.

General Sheridan had brought to the front all his troops, and established them on the line which he found General [George Washington] Getty holding.

General Merritt with his cavalry division was posted on the left of Getty, and on the extreme left of the line; On Getty's right were the other divisions of the Sixth Corps (General [Horatio G.] Wright); then came the Nineteenth Corps (General [William H.] Emory); next, and on the extreme right, was posted General [George Armstrong] Custer's cavalry division.

All being in readiness, the Commanding General leaped his horse over the temporary defence of rails and fresh earth, and with his headquarters flag in hand, and followed by his staff, rode along the entire front of his army, amid hearty cheers and enthusiastic demonstrations from the troops. Then at the word a general advance took place, while the demoralized Confederates fell back pell-mell. The Union infantry halted on the line of Cedar Creek and reoccupied the camps from which they had been so unceremoniously driven. The cavalry pressed the enemy closely, and before they rested, had recaptured the twenty-four guns and ambulances taken by Early in the morning, together with twenty-four guns and fifty-six ambulances belonging to the Confederates. Many battle-flags and twelve hundred prisoners were among the other spoils of war.

This was the last serious effort on the part of the Confederates to hold the Valley. Sheridan had already rendered it untenable for an army, by destroying the crops, and soon after both belligerents quitted the scene of so many struggles.

The battle of Cedar Creek was one of the notable military episodes of modern times, and a brilliant illustration of the wondrous power possessed and exercised at a critical moment by a born leader of men!

1. "The Shenandoah Valley" by G. E. Pond. New York: Scribner's and Sons, 1883.

# Gettysburg

America's true title to liberty was written in blood upon the battle-field of Gettysburg. There, on the free soil of Pennsylvania, Slavery received the death-wound from which life ebbed away.

The closing act of that bloody drama of three days' duration, the repulse of Pickett's charge, the artist M. de Thulstrup has here portrayed to us in vivid colors. For two days the battle had raged along the entire lines of both armies, with varying results. On the third day Gen. [Robert E.] Lee prepared his forces for this last great struggle, which was to break, if possible, the Union lines at the centre, and thus divide the army of Gen. [George Gordon] Meade. The spot indicated by the "clump of trees" was selected as the point upon which the assault should be made. This portion of our line, on which this terrible storm was soon to break, was held by [General Alexander Stewart] Webb's brigade (the Philadelphia brigade), of the Second Division, Second Corps. It was then posted in front of the battle-line shown in the picture, along the line of the low stone wall, which is about one hundred feet in front of the troops here meeting the final attack. On the left was the 69th Pennsylvania; on their right two companies of the 106th (the remainder of the regiment had been sent to the right to assist [General O. O.] Howard); thence the wall was left open for the fire of artillery from Cushing and Brown; then a portion

66

In this sketch is shown that portion of the battle ground over which Pickett's charge was made. The "clump of trees" at the left was the point of direction for Pickett's forces. The monument is that of Webb's brigade, near which Gen. Webb was wounded; to the right, in the distance, is seen the Codori House. (From a photograph by Tipton.)

of the 71st Regiment (its left wing); then behind the low stone wall (shown in the sketch) was the right wing of the 71st; and finally the 72d, in line about one hundred feet in rear of the position in which it is now fighting.

The time here represented is about 3 o'clock in the afternoon of July 3, 1863, when [Confederate General Lewis A.] Armistead, leading the advance of [General George E.] Pickett's division, had forced back a portion of the 71st Regiment Pennsylvania Volunteers to the line assumed by the 72d Regiment, and had crowned the low stone wall which served to mark out the line of defence assumed by Webb's brigade.[1]

In the picture are shown the troops of Webb's command, the enemy's attacking column, and, on the extreme left, the advance of Col. Hall's re-enforcements, the Third Brigade of the Second Division. In the centre foreground Gen. [Winfield Scott] Hancock, with his headquarters staff, appears. During the engagement he was wounded, but to the left of this line of battle. At the right is seen the reserve artillery coming into action to relieve the shattered batteries of Cushing and Brown.

The line of battle presented in this picture extends from the angle of the fence in the foreground (as shown in the pen-and-ink sketch), past the monument, including the "clump of trees," towards the Round-Tops. The angle at which the view is given is shown by following from the point where Gen. Armistead is presented to us, the line of battle-flags to the extreme right of the picture; which line of advance was nearly perpendicular to our line of defence.

A sharp engagement on the extreme right in the early dawn of this, the third day, was followed by lesser demonstrations along the lines until 10 o'clock in the forenoon. Then ensued an ominous silence,—a calm before the coming storm. One hundred thousand men in arms, within sight and short cannon range of each other, are awaiting the command that shall plunge them into this arena in deadly strife. During this lull in hostilities, Gen. Lee is arranging his army for the desperate charge which is soon to follow. The attacking columns were formed to the right of that portion of Seminary Ridge which is seen in the picture, and consisted of Pickett's division, supported on the right by [Cadmus M.] Wilcox, on the left by [Henry] Heth's division under [James J.] Pettigrew and

---

1. It will be perceived that it was not a very difficult thing for the head of the column *to pass over the stone wall* and to enter the open space in front of Webb's ranks, if the men could be forced to come up to the remaining guns of Cushing and the fresh guns of Cowan's New York battery, which had hurried up to replace Cushing and Brown, whose batteries were then masses of débris. (The artist has withdrawn from in front of the 72d Regiment, Generals Webb, Armistead, and Cushing, in order to introduce them in this view.)

[William D.] Pender, with Wright's brigade as reserves in the rear. This force numbered about eighteen thousand men. Pickett's division, comprising the brigades of Armistead, [James L.] Kemper, and [Richard B.] Garnett,—in all, fifteen Virginia regiments of tried veterans, distinguished for discipline and valor,—had arrived fresh upon the field. This division was selected to lead the great assault.

At 1 o'clock P.M. two guns were fired in quick succession, and instantly the roar of one hundred and fifty cannon along the Confederate lines answered this signal, the shot and shell from their terrific fire sweeping like a tornado through the Union ranks on Cemetery Ridge. The main fury of this cannonade fell upon the foreground shown in the picture, where were planted Cushing's Battery A of the 4th U. S. Artillery, and Brown's Rhode Island Battery. On the left of these were stationed Cowan and Rorty, and on the right of the Second Corps line, Arnold's and Woodruff's batteries were located. During this storm of shot and shell, every gun of these batteries that was not disabled was handled with precision and vigor, and not a cannoneer left his post.

For an hour and a half this artillery combat continued its terrible destruction,—the most severe cannonading ever witnessed,—when Generals Meade and Hunt gave orders for our artillery to cease firing, well knowing that such an attack as we were about to experience would certainly follow this evidence of strength and accuracy of the enemy's artillery fire.

It was then that Lee, lured on by the apparent weakness of our artillery fire, issued the order which was to start Pickett on his mission. [General James] Longstreet had not agreed with his commander, knowing well, from long experience, that the troops which were to meet his attack were not demoralized from the effects of the previous days' fighting, nor from the artillery fire through which they had just passed. He hesitated to give the final word ordering the advance, and turned aside his head. Pickett, accepting his silence for consent, saluted and said, " I am going to move forward, sir." Soon his division appears crossing the Emmettsburg road, sweeping on into the open field, beyond which is the centre of the Army of the Potomac.

Gen. Webb himself thus describes the charge:—

"At about 2:45 P.M., Pickett's column, in as fine order as if going to dress-parade, quiet, well drilled, well commanded, in fact veterans of the Peninsula, of Fredericksburg, and Antietam, moved grandly forward.

"Pickett and Pettigrew and [Isaac R.] Trimble—Virginia and Georgia and North Carolina, Virginia leading—are to take this clump of trees. See them now as their lines descend towards us—our countrymen, but our foes. We cannot be other than proud of our enemies. They come to crown this crest, or perish.

"Two lines of regiments, possibly eighteen thousand men, are moving on our line slowly and determinedly. They near the crest. Cushing, wounded, asks to have his remaining gun run down to the fence, and (glorious martyr), wounded, yea, sorely, stands by that piece, the very picture of a soldier. Americans can well glory in the achievements of the Cushings. But Hancock, our glorious Hancock, ever near the front in action, was not to be easily overthrown by this mass of angry foes. He had the old Second Corps and [General Abner] Doubleday's division of the First; and well he knew how, to use us! [George J.] Stannard was to be used to stay the supporting column on the Rebel right, and well he did it. Gates, of [Thomas A.] Rowley's First Brigade, was enabled to assist in this movement. Harrow and Hall, of our own division, were near to help us, and Hays on our right with the Third Division, with Smith's brigade, was well able to hold his own.

"On, on they come with solid front! line closing in upon line, as their right or left felt the pressure of Hancock's aggressive movements. And now they strike the 69th, under Col. O'Kane, and a portion of the 71st, under Lieut.-Col.

Kochersperger, and, halting under the withering fire of these brave men, pressed toward the open part of the wall, in front of the space held formerly by Cushing. Here, Armistead, waving his sword aloft, had rushed in with his men. Here, Cushing had died at his piece. Here, was to be the final struggle for the crest! But this crest was not to be taken from us, if, by self-sacrifice and by individual effort, it could be retained.

"Pressed by a wedge-shaped column, the right of those who guarded the wall on the left of Cushing was pressed to the rear, but not penetrated or driven to the rear. They were better for defence in their new position. The brigade commander himself pointed out to them the number of Rebels who had passed to their right, and directed them to fire upon them, and to fight their right and rear.

"But past the wall—low enough for Armistead to step over—what had they to meet? First, from our right the fire of the companies of the 71st under Col. R. Penn Smith; then from the front the fire of the 72d Regiment, perfectly organized and in line on this crest, and from our left and left centre that of the body of Hall's men, the guard or rear guard under Capt. Ford and Lieut. Lynch of the 106th, which hurried to be with their brigade in the fray, and finally, also, the rush of Kochersperger's men. Armistead dying, their dead and wounded within our lines (killed and maimed in a hand-to-

69

70

hand contest), pressed right and left, with no hope of success in their front, and no hope of retreat, they surrendered. Hall, Hays, and Harrow did much to aid in securing this result; in every battle it will be and has been in vain to try to claim all the praise and all success for any one brigade or regiment; but I defy you to find a contest in which any one brigade performed more nobly the part assigned to it."[2]

Col. Banes, in his narrative, says of this moment:—

"The battle rages most furiously. Armistead, with a hundred and fifty of his Virginians, is inside our lines, only a few paces from our brigade-commander; they look each other in the face,—Union men are intermingled with the enemy,—rifles, bayonets, and clubbed muskets are freely used and men on both sides rapidly fall. The struggle lasts but a few minutes, when the enemy in front throw down their arms, and rushing through the lines of the 72d Regiment, hasten to the rear as prisoners without a guard; while others of the column who might have escaped, unwilling to risk a retreat over the path by which they came, surrender. Gen. Webb won the esteem of his men for his skilful management, and for the extraordinary coolness displayed in the midst of danger. At the time the

Confederate leader, Armistead, fell, Webb received a wound; but, concealing it from those around him, continued on duty."

In alluding to this scene, when presenting to Gen. Webb a bronze medal as a fitting testimonial of his appreciation of the example Webb had furnished the army on this occasion, Gen. Meade thus wrote:—

"In selecting those to whom I should distribute these medals, I know no one general who has more claims than yourself, either 'for distinguished personal gallantry on that ever-memorable field,' or for the cordial, warm, and generous sympathy and support so grateful for a commanding general to receive from his subordinates."

Col. Banes, the assistant adjutant-general, carried Webb's brigade colors, and was everywhere among the regiments, and it is not surprising that he is claimed to be with each regiment in their several histories.

Gen. Webb in his report says :—

"The brigade captured nearly one thousand prisoners and six battle-flags and picked up fourteen hundred stand of arms and nine hundred sets of accoutrements. The loss was forty-three officers and four hundred and fifty-two men, and *only forty-seven* were missing."

2. Extract from Gen. A. S. Webb's oration at the dedication of the 72d Pennsylvania Regiment's Monument at Gettysburg, July, 1883.

1. Flag of 3d Brigade, 2d Division, 2d Corps.
2. Flag of 20th Mass. Vols.
3. Flag of 42d New York Vols.
4. Col. Norman J. Hall, commanding 3d Brigade.
5. Maj. Wm. G. Mitchell, Aid to Gen. Hancock.
6. Colors of Headquarters, 2d Corps.
7. Brig.-Gen. Alexander Stewart Webb, commanding 2d Brigade.
8. Colors of 2d Brigade, 2d Division, 2d Corps.
9. Lieut. A. H. Cushing, commanding Battery A, 4th U. S. Artillery.
10. Brig.-Gen. L. A. Armistead, commanding Brigade, Pickett's Division.

11. Capt. Chas. Banes, Adjutant-General 2d Brigade.
12. Capt. Henry L. Abbott, commanding 20th Mass.
13. Maj.-Gen. W. S. Hancock, commanding 2d Corps.
14. Lieut. G. Verplanck Weir, Battery C, 5th U. S. Artillery.
15. Lieut.-Col. Theodore Hesser, commanding 72d Penn. Vols.
16. Color Guard 72d Penn. Vols.
17. Disabled Guns, Cushing's Battery.
18. Codori House.
19. Reserve Artillery.
C, C, C.  Location of Cowan's Battery

The regiments before us had lost eighteen officers and many enlisted men during the attack made upon their line at 6:30 P.M., on the 2d inst., when Brown's Rhode Island battery was captured and again retaken. This attack had been made on their left, and the struggle had been severe,—the enemy coming in hot haste, encouraged by their success in outflanking and overwhelming the stanch and reliable troops of the Third Corps.

At the moment here represented Cushing's battery had been almost destroyed. The single piece commanded by Sergt. Fuger is doing its last work. Cowan's First New York Independent Battery is in position on the left of Cushing, holding the place previously held by Brown's battery, now disabled and out of ammunition. Canister is being hurled into the enemy's ranks from six or seven field-pieces. Stannard's Vermont men have taken a position to the front of and perpendicular to our line of battle, and are pouring in their flank fire upon Pickett's right; on his left, Pettigrew's brigades are engaged in a hot contest with the troops of Hay's division.

The troops here meeting the charge of the impetuous foe from that day are known in history as the "Philadelphia Brigade," which held their lines against the enemy's hosts until their comrades could rush in *en masse* to help them.

This picture, therefore, is of historic value, and of great interest to all who were with, and who glory in, the achievements of the Army of the Potomac. Those taking part in that hand-to-hand struggle are representative men of that army, and are doing what their comrades would have done had they been posted at the "clump of trees." As Gen. Hancock said, "They held the spot every true soldier would have desired to hold."

When Armistead, swinging his hat on his sword, cried, "Boys, give them the cold steel!" that moment "the highest wave of the rebellion had reached its farthest limit, ever after to recede." Before another force could dash itself against that line of blue, the last attack of Lee at Gettysburg had been repulsed.

# BATTLE OF

## *Antietam*

At the close of the battle of South Mountain, which was, take it all round, a brilliant victory for the Union troops, General Robert E. Lee is said to have remarked, "We (the Confederates) have lost fifteen thousand men in battle and by desertion since we crossed the Potomac, and have been forced from a very strong position, from which I did not believe it possible for the Federal Army to dislodge us." A retreat was necessary; and Lee, gathering up his beaten and disheartened columns, pushed on, and was but a few hours later followed by the victorious Unionists. The enemy had re-enforcements, or would be joined by re-enforcements of the six divisions which had assisted in the capture of Harper's Ferry, but to the Unionists no re-enforcements were to arrive. Often the rear of the enemy and our own advance would come in conflict, but the engagements were very slight and led to no results. At nightfall on the 15th of September, 1862, Lee had his retreating divisions in line of battle behind the Antietam, while our own troops were forming on the opposite side of the stream, though as yet they had taken up no proper offensive or defensive position. In the front of the left wing of the Union Army, a stone bridge crossed the Antietam; near the centre was a second bridge; and opposite the right wing was an easily crossed ford for infantry, while at various parts of the stream it was practicable for the crossing of artillery and cavalry.

74

The following day was one of much inactivity, certainly with the Union troops, and there appeared to be great delay in selecting and assigning positions. With the enemy, everything was in activity, and to give the greater inspiration, Stonewall Jackson with his forces was hastening to the spot from which he scented the battle, and joined his chief early on the 16th with four of his divisions, the other four arriving the following day. The Union troops, with the exception of three detached divisions under General [William B.] Franklin, were all within striking distance of the enemy, whose position was well known, but nevertheless there was an unaccountable delay in the formation of our lines.

About three o'clock on the afternoon of the 16th, Hooker's corps of the Union Army crossed the Antietam by the upper bridge, demonstrating against the left of the Confederates on the Hagerstown pike, and advanced in a westerly direction. A mile and more north of the Dunker Church, and in a cornfield, [General Joseph] Hooker struck Hood's division, made up of Texans, with whom he had a sharp encounter, which resulted in expelling the enemy, and the establishment of Hooker's lines in the cornfield near Hoffman's house, and the throwing out of pickets. Hood's division was now thrown to the rear of the Dunker Church, while [Richard S.] Ewell's division was placed in position to confront Hooker, who had been joined during the night by the Twelfth Corps under [General Joseph K. F.] Mansfield. The following day, the 17th, was to prove the great day of battle.

The Confederates, who had extended their lines to a distance of more than four miles across a bend of the Potomac, upon which both their flanks rested, were well posted, and during the early part of the day their front line was maintained along the Hagerstown pike, running north and south, and in the adjacent cornfields and timber, where severe fighting occurred. With the right wing of the Confederates were Colonel Lee's batteries, and with the left, Stewart's horse artillery, which occupied ridges commanding all the open fields across which the Federal troops would find it necessary to march to the attack. Other artillery was placed at every coigne of vantage along the entire line.

With day dawn, [General George B.] McClellan developed his plan of battle. Hooker was to assault directly in his front and turn the left flank of the enemy. Sumner's corps, which was at Kedysville, was to march straight across the open fields, attack and endeavor to crush the enemy's left centre near the Dunker Church. [General Ambrose E.] Burnside was to make a grand assault, regardless of loss, and carry the bridge in his front, force the enemy's lines beyond, and push through the

Confederate right wing to the Shepardstown pike, south of Sharpsburg. Either one of these movements proving successful would result in a decisive victory for the Union; with all successful, the army of the Confederacy would be annihilated.

At five o'clock in the morning, the Confederate batteries opened upon Hooker, who replied. At daylight, Meade with his division moved through the belt of woods and opened a musketry fire, which the enemy sharply returned. The Federal troops were falling fast, but the line pushed on amid the weakening fire of the enemy. [James B.] Ricketts, with two brigades, now came up on Meade's left, and the long line swept on, pursuing the Confederates, who were making for the woods in the rear of the Dunker Church. The Union troops pushed on, nearly to the Hagerstown pike, where Hooker was met by Stonewall Jackson's old division and by Hood's Texans. Under cover of the woods, Jackson delivered a heavy fire, while [J. E. B.] Stuart's horse artillery delivered a stubborn cross fire upon the Union works, which created some slight confusion in Hooker's lines, taking advantage of which, Jackson threw forward his whole line. For a moment the Federal line halted, and then fled back to the cover of the woods, from whence they had driven the enemy but a few moments previously. Fresh troops were now summoned to the front, and the retreat of

Hooker's line was stayed, Jackson's advance was met, and a furious Federal fire hurled against it. It was now Jackson's time to hesitate, and his line turned and fled to the wood behind the Hagerstown pike and near to the Dunker Church. Now, Hooker opened his batteries, and under their murderous fire advanced, but succeeded in only reaching a few hundred feet beyond and to the north of the pike. Meade's Pennsylvania Reserves became demoralized; for so intent was Hooker upon pushing his attack with his First Corps, that the Twelfth Corps, under Mansfield, was not called into action until now, when his own troops had been badly broken up. At a little later than seven in the morning, Hooker called on the Twelfth Corps for assistance, and the response was immediate.

Mansfield faced to the south in line of battle, and gallantly advanced along the east side of the Hagerstown pike, where they were met by [John Bell] Hood's Texans, re-enforced by four fresh brigades. The enemy was encountered in the open field, over which Meade had fought at sunrise. The conflict raged for a time, but in the end the Federals were victorious and swept the enemy from the field. Twice already, thus early in the day, had the same ground been fought over and won. Three hours had now elapsed. Union and Confederates re-formed their lines, but neither of them seemed inclined to

76

continue the contest. The Federal advance was established near the Hagerstown pike, about a half-mile north of the wood where the Dunker Church was situated. In this severe conflict, General Mansfield, shortly after going into action, was mortally wounded; and General Hooker was painfully wounded and obliged to retire from the field.

The enemy's lines, near the Dunker Church, was the key to the Confederate position, and this position was assailed by the Second Corps, the three divisions of which had passed the night on the left bank of the Antietam. At seven o'clock, while the First and Twelfth Corps were hotly engaged, two divisions of the Second pushed across the river and moved against the enemy's left centre, near the Dunker Church. Sumner was in command of the corps. He formed each of his divisions with three lines of brigade front. To reach the enemy he was obliged now to move forward a mile and a half or more. French's division diverged too far to the south, and was brought to a stand in front of the church. [John] Sedgewick's division, led by Sumner, moved steadily to the westward. The Confederates opened upon it with artillery with terrible effect; but onward it swept, and was soon under a galling musketry fire. At length a halt was called, and a burst of musketry told that the enemy had made a stand on the turnpike and was hotly engaged with the lead-

ing brigade. For half an hour the battle was kept up, when the rebels broke and retreated. Sumner swept on, crossed the pike, passed the Dunker Church, and continued the advance until the first line entered the wood, when the command was again halted, and another contest entered upon by the leading brigade and the enemy, who shortly fell back to the opposite side of the woods, half a mile west of Dunker Church, and made a final stand. Again Sumner advanced until the opposing foes were within two hundred yards of each other, and here the battle raged with terrible slaughter.

General Lee had made new arrangements of his forces, and disposed them around the Dunker Church in order to check the Federal advance on its left flank. It was now ten o'clock in the morning, and seven fresh brigades of the enemy were advancing from the south upon the exposed left flank of Sedgwick's hitherto victorious division, which should have been protected had not French moved too far to the south. Of a sudden, Sedgwick heard musketry in his left and rear. A confusion among the Federal troops took place, and in a brief space of time Sedgwick's splendid division melted away after doing deeds of desperate valor. What was left of it retired in good order towards the right of the field of battle, and about five hundred yards farther north formed a new line, nearly perpendicular to the Hagerstown pike. New dispositions were made to fill the gap created by Sedgwick's discomfiture. A gallant but unsuccessful attempt was made to recapture the position, and with this the fighting on the Federal right practically ended. The enemy retained the woods, but under an incessant and furious cannonade of the Union artillery on the right and centre. Sedgwick's division, about five thousand strong, lost more than two thousand men, but not a color was taken, nor a prisoner, save those helplessly wounded.

Of the final result of the bloody battle of Antietam, every one is aware. It is with the operations around the Dunker Church that we have more particularly to do, that being the subject of our illustration.

# *Spotsylvania*

## AND THE BLOODY ANGLE

The battle—or rather let it be said, that series of conflicts known as the battle—of Spotsylvania Court House makes one of the bloodiest pictures of the book of time. After the unsatisfactory fight in the Wilderness, General [Ulysses S.] Grant, finding the enemy well intrenched, continued his operations by a movement on their left flank, with the hope of bringing on an engagement in more open country, and under more favorable surroundings.

In accordance with his determination, General Grant directed Major-General George G. Meade, who was the immediate commander of the Army of the Potomac, to take possession, by a night march, of Spotsylvania Court House, which

movement, let it be said, was merely preliminary, and in a great measure dependent upon the operations of General Lee, to a further movement in a still more northerly direction. The army began its movement at half past eight on the evening of the 7th of May, 1864. The enemy early became apprised of the movement, and commenced counter-operations. At one o'clock, on the morning of the 8th, General Merritt with his cavalry was directed to advance his command beyond Spotsylvania Court House, with a view of clearing all the roads, and when, at five o'clock in the morning, General Warren with the Fifth Corps had reached where General Merritt's headquarters had been, about a mile east of Todd's Tavern on the Brock road, he informed General Meade that General Merritt had been for some time engaged. Merritt had encountered General Fitzhugh Lee's division of rebel cavalry, which had barricaded the road. Merritt could make but little progress, and in a short time General Warren ordered an advance of his infantry corps to his assistance. But the character of the ground was such as greatly to impede the movements of the infantry. At about half past eight, however, Warren's troops, [John C.] Robinson's division leading, broke from the woods into open ground about two miles and a half from the Court House. At this point there was a fork of the Brock road, which united again after the distance of a mile. Robinson took the fork to the left, and reaching the junction of the forks, he re-formed his division in line of regiments, and advancing along the road in open ground, was received by a severe fire of musketry and artillery from an intrenchment in the woods. They fell back for shelter to the woods in their rear, their commanding officer, General Robinson, being severely wounded in the first fire. In the mean time, General [Charles] Griffin, commanding the First Division of Warren's corps, marching along the road, met with the same results as did Robinson's men; but by the personal exertions of Griffin and his brigade commanders, the men quickly reformed, scattering the enemy, and took up a line which they held for several days. Griffin was followed by Cutler's division, and the whole corps was now intrenched, distant from two hundred to four hundred yards from the position of the enemy.

General Hancock, with his Second Corps, followed Warren's corps from his position in the Wilderness, as far as Todd's Tavern, when he relieved Gregg's division of cavalry, and the corps was placed in position and intrenched. The march of all the troops was a very distressing one on account of the intense heat and burning woods of the Wilderness, as well as the thick dust, which caused an intolerable craving for water.

Some time about one o'clock in the afternoon of the 8th, General Sedgwick, with the Sixth Corps, was directed to move to Spotsylvania Court House, and unite with Warren in an immediate and strong attack upon the enemy's lines, and of this movement General Hancock was duly notified. It was late in the afternoon when the arrangements for the combined attack of the Fifth and Sixth Corps were fully completed, and, as the troops were tired out, the attack was lacking in force, and in no wise successful. The day following was given up to a much-needed rest, and no operations were undertaken, save the necessary ones of readjusting and strengthening the lines, and placing additional artillery in position. It was this morning, while overlooking the work of his men on their intrenchments, that the brave General John Sedgwick, of the Sixth Corps, was killed by a rebel sharp-shooter.

Burnside, with his Ninth Corps, had orders to move from his position in the Wilderness to Piney Branch Church; but early on the 8th, he was directed to make a halt before reaching that position. Early on the morning of the 9th, he left his halting-place at Aldrich's, and moved by way of the Orange and Fredericksburg plank road in the direction of the Court House, in his march encountering a force of dismounted cavalry and a brigade of Longstreet's troops.

Burnside's report to General Grant, that he had encountered a force on the Fredericksburg road, caused an order to be given to General Hancock to examine the river Po, with a view to its passage. In accordance with his instructions, his three commanders, [David Bell] Birney, [Francis] Barlow, and [John] Gibbon, crossed the stream at three different points. General Birney met with considerable resistance, and, after the troops had crossed, three pontoon bridges were laid. The column was pushed forward, but darkness and dense woods interposed, and a halt for the night was called. The next day, Hancock was directed to ascertain the position and force of the enemy in his front, especially the location of his left flank, and to hold his corps in readiness for an advance against the enemy, while the troops of the Sixth Corps were to do likewise. The dawn had scarcely begun to manifest itself on the morning of the 10th, when Hancock made a minute examination of the Block House Bridge, and found the enemy in strong force on the opposite bank, inside intrenchments, which commanded the bridge and its approaches. In this state of affairs, he sent a brigade farther down the river to ascertain what could be accomplished there. Just at this moment, he received a despatch from General Meade directing him to transfer two of his divisions to Warren's position, and arrange with Warren to make a vigorous attack on the line of the enemy at five o'clock, and, in virtue of seniority, Hancock was to command all the troops which should be engaged.

Hancock examined the ground where the attack was to be. When Birney's division was withdrawn across the Po, some of his regiments were attacked near Glady Run, and driven in, showing that the enemy were advancing in force. General Meade, being informed of this, directed Barlow's division to be withdrawn from the southerly side of the Po also. While this withdrawal was in progress, Heth's rebel division of [Confederate General A. P.] Hill's corps advanced and attacked the brigades of Brooke and Brown, which were to the right and rear of the brigades of Mills and Smith, with great vigor. The enemy, however, were met with a well-directed and destructive fire, and they fell back with a heavy loss. For a second time they advanced. So incessant was the musketry and cannonading that the woods took fire, and the two brigades of Brooke and Brown crossed the river. This crossing emboldened the enemy, and again they advanced under a terrific artillery fire, which swept the ground in all directions; but they were checked, and retired disheartened. Many of our wounded were burned by the fire in the woods. Additional intrenchments were now made on the enemy's left.

It was known that various attacks were to be made on the afternoon of the 10th, and all through the morning there was sharp skirmish and artillery fire. About half past three, Hancock was informed that General Warren considered the opportunity favorable for an immediate attack in force, and Gibbon's division of Hancock's corps was directed to co-operate with Warren, while Wright of the Sixth Corps, with Mott's division, was at a quarter of four directed to attack immediately. General Warren commenced the assault with two of his divisions, and two brigades of Gibbon's. The attack was made through a dense wood of cedar-trees which was in front of the intrenchments of the enemy, which made it most difficult for our troops to advance under the heavy fire of the rebels. But advance they did, and finally reached the open ground near the intrenchments, though with somewhat disordered ranks. It absolutely hailed cannon-balls and bullets. Yet our brave lads were not dismayed;

for they straightened their lines and pushed forward. Some of them reached the abatis in front of the intrenchments; some penetrated to the very crest of the parapet. Of what avail? They could not stand against the heavy fire, and all were driven back with a great loss. The attack was renewed at seven o'clock, with Birney's and Gibbon's divisions of the Second Corps and part of the Fifth Corps, but it was no more successful.

Meanwhile General Wright, of the Sixth Corps, discovered a part of the enemy's works which he regarded as vulnerable. A column of attack was formed under the command of Colonel Upton, and General [Gershom] Mott, with his division, who was placed under the orders of General Wright, was likewise directed to be ready to assault the works in his immediate front at five P.M. Colonel Upton's column rushed forward to the attack, under a terrible fire from front and flank, gained the parapet of the works, had a desperate hand-to-hand encounter of a few moments' duration, swarmed in over the works and captured a large number of prisoners; pressing forward, he reached the second line of intrenchments, and its defending battery was captured. The enemy's line was completely broken, but owing to the non-arrival of Mott's division, which was to have supported the left, and re-enforcements arriving to the enemy, they were ordered to withdraw under cover of the darkness. Upton made a gallant assault, capturing near twelve hundred prisoners and several stand of colors. It won for him his brigadier's star. In some respects, the day all round was disastrous to us, for General [James Clay] Rice, of Cutler's division of the Fifth Corps, was mortally wounded, and General Thomas Stevenson, commanding a division of the Ninth Corps, was killed while making a reconnaissance on the Court House.

At three o'clock, on the afternoon of the 11th, General Meade was directed by General Grant to "move three divisions of the Second Corps by the rear of the Fifth and Sixth Corps, under cover of the night, so as to join the Ninth Corps in a vigorous assault on the enemy, at four o'clock A.M., tomorrow." The Fifth and Sixth Corps were already as close to the enemy as was considered judicious, either for assaulting or for withdrawing to attack elsewhere, but both the commanders of these corps were directed to have their troops in readiness at four o'clock, for the combined attack of Burnside and Hancock, when they might possibly be required. Hancock's troops, in a heavy rain, reached the designated point, at the Brown house, about twelve hundred yards from the enemy's intrenchments, at half past twelve o'clock. Here there was more open ground,— about four hundred yards in width; and, opposite this opening, Barlow's division was formed in two lines massed. In the front of General Birney's division there was a marsh and a thick wood of stunted pines. Gibbon's division was in reserve, in the rear. The fog was so heavy that it was pitch dark, and General Hancock postponed the hour of attack until shortly after half past four, when word was given to advance. When about half-way up to the enemy's intrenchments, and on the open ground, the troops in column and line gave a resounding cheer, and with an impetuous rush, that nothing could check, dashed through the abatis, scaled the intrenchments, took nearly four thousand prisoners, thirty pieces of artillery, with caissons and horses complete, several thousand stand of small arms, and over twenty colors; and, among the prisoners, were Major-General Edward Johnson and Brigadier-General Geo. H. Stewart. There was, moreover, a heavy loss to the rebels in killed and wounded. Our victorious troops pursued the enemy until a second line of intrenchments was encountered. The troops held in reserve occupied the already captured works of the enemy. By six o'clock in the morning, General Meade was made aware of General Hancock's successes, with such information of the attempts of the enemy to assume offensive measures, that Wright, with the Sixth Corps, was ordered to move forward, and attack at once on Hancock's right. Moving with two divisions, which were in readiness, he pushed forward to the west angle of the salient of the works which had been captured, and relieved the Second Corps troops there. General Wright was wounded shortly after coming up, but, nevertheless, he would not relinquish the command of his men. As soon as he arrived he commenced a very strong attack from the apex of the west angle and the thick pine wood and swamps before mentioned, but quite close up to the west face of the salient; and it was in the immediate vicinity that the close and deadly fighting of "The Bloody Angle," which is the subject of our picture, took place, and which continued with the greatest fury until near dark, and was kept up with some abatement until three o'clock the following morning, when the enemy fell back upon a new line of intrenchment, which had been built during the night.

At this west angle the fighting was literally of the bloodiest description. It may be that during the entire war there was no more severe hand-to-hand conflict. Brigadier-General [Lewis A.] Grant, who commanded the Vermont brigade of the Second Division of the Sixth Corps, and who was ordered to relieve General Barlow's division of the Second Corps, one of the most gallant participants in this struggle to the death, speaking of it with all the certainty of one who knows, says: "It was not only a desperate struggle, but it was literally a hand-to-hand fight. Nothing but the piled-up logs or breastworks separated the combatants. Our men would reach over the logs and fire into the faces of the enemy, would stab over with their bayonets; many were shot and stabbed through the crevices and holes between the logs; men mounted the works, and with muskets rapidly handed them, kept up a continuous fire until they were shot down, when others would take their places and continue the deadly work. Several times, during the day, the rebels would show a white flag about the works, and when our fire slackened, jump over and surrender, and others were crowded down to fill their places. It was there that the somewhat celebrated tree was cut off by bullets; there that the brush and logs were cut to pieces, and whipped into basket-stuff; there that the rebel ditches and cross sections were filled with dead men several deep. I was at the angle next day; the sight was terrible and sickening, much worse than at Bloody Lane (Antietam). There a great many dead men were lying in the road and across the rails of the torn-down fences, and out in the cornfield; but they were not piled up several deep, and their flesh was not so torn and mangled as at the angle." The carnage was terrible. General [Samuel] McGowan, of the Confederate troops, says: "Our men lay on one side of the breastworks, the enemy on the other, and, in many instances, men were pulled over"; and he further adds: "The trenches, on the right, in the bloody angle, had to be cleared of the dead more than once. An oak tree, twenty-two inches in diameter, in rear of the brigade, was cut down by musket-balls, and fell about twelve o'clock, Thursday night, injuring several men in the First South Carolina Regiment."

But while this deadly work was going on, our other troops were by no means inactive. General Warren, early on the morning of the 12th, opened with all his artillery, and pushed his skirmish line forward. At quarter past nine he was ordered to attack at once, and with his whole force, if deemed necessary. He made an assault, and was repulsed by Longstreet's corps, which was holding the intrenchments in his front. Longstreet says that Warren made "two violent assaults." His attacks failing, he was ordered to send Cutler's division to the assistance of General Wright, and to be ready to follow with the remainder of his corps. It appeared possible that the enemy's intrenchments in the vicinity of the ''Bloody Angle'' could be carried, if assaulted by the entire Fifth Corps; so Griffin's division immediately followed Cutler, and the rest of the corps were following when the contemplated assault was abandoned. On the left of our line, General [Robert B.] Potter's division of Burnside's corps, at four o'clock, on the morning of the 12th, advanced against the enemy's intrenchments.

Those Potter carried about an hour later, and captured in them some prisoners and two guns. The rebel commander, Lane, re-formed his brigade in some old intrenchments, which enfiladed Potter, drove him out, and recaptured the guns. Some time after nine o'clock, Potter succeeded in establishing a connection with Hancock, and skirmishing and heavy artillery firing were kept up throughout all Burnside's corps, until late in the day. Early on the morning of the 13th, it having been learned that the enemy had withdrawn from the salient, the various corps pressed forward, when it was found that the enemy were three quarters of a mile in the rear of the apex of the salient in a very strongly intrenched line, which was occupied by infantry and artillery.

This brought to a close the scenes of great fights around Spotsylvania Court House. General Grant was determined to fight it out on this line, and again the order was "By the left flank, march," the movement promising an opportunity of attacking the Confederates on their right flank, before they could be re-enforced from their left, or their intrenchments extended. At the same time, the movement would cover our hospitals and our depots of supplies at Washington. This movement was attended with more or less fighting, there being quite a sharp action on the 18th of May. But the movement by the left flank was kept up, the object being to effect a lodgement on the southerly bank of the James River.

# Chattanooga

Among the more important struggles for the preservation of the Union on the one hand, and its dismemberment on the other, none stands out in a bolder or more picturesque light than the battle of Chattanooga, Tenn., which was fought Nov. 22-25, 1863, between the Confederates under [Braxton] Bragg, and the Union forces commanded by Grant.

The opposing armies comprised the flower of American youth, seasoned by the experience of several campaigns, and organized, disciplined, and led by generals who had won their grades, in most cases, at the cannon's mouth, and who, in at least three instances, were destined to tread the topmost round of the ladder of military fame. But here the parallel ends. The Confederates were equal if not superior in numbers, well supplied with food, and occupying a position of great natural strength, made well-nigh impregnable by earthworks, rising tier above tier, on the eastern and southern side of the Union lines; while on their west and north, nearly all communication with the outer world was closed. The Union troops had been for some time on half rations, and were reduced to sharing the corn with their draught animals, of which more than ten thousand perished of starvation during the campaign. The troops had also suffered reverses at Chickamauga, and were somewhat dispirited. It seemed a mere question of days when the gray eagle soaring over the besieged force would swoop down upon the gaunt and hungry bluecoats in the valley.

The venerable saying, "Brag is a good dog, but Holdfast's a better one," was nevertheless to be again verified. General [George H.] Thomas had officially reported, while yet Grant was afar off, "We will hold the town till we starve!"

At the time of the battle the situation was as follows: The town of Chattanooga, with a nominal population of 5,000, was nestled in one of the numerous curves for which the Tennessee River is noted, and on its eastern bank. Opposite the town, on the east, and about three miles distant, ran a mountainous range, five hundred feet high, and fairly covered with timber; this was called Missionary Ridge. Southwest of Chattanooga towered Lookout Mountain, fifteen hundred feet above the river level. Both of these imposing positions were occupied by the Confederates, while half-way between these points and the town a line of temporary works had been erected on high ground by the Union troops. On this line were several detached crests or knolls; one of these, in the centre and about equidistant between the town and Missionary Ridge, is called Orchard Knob. Above the town and connecting the line of Missionary Ridge with the Tennessee River, is Chickamauga Creek, while farther to the southward and nearly parallel to the creek was the

embankment of the Chattanooga and Cleveland Railroad, which penetrated the northern extremity of the ridge by a tunnel. The ground lying between the ridge and the town was known as Chattanooga Valley, from the stream which runs through its centre.

Upon assuming command, General Grant first gave attention to a plan initiated by General Thomas to open communication with Nashville via Bridgeport, a station on the railroad to which access had hitherto been barred by the enemy. This plan, with some modifications, was approved, and in a few days additional supplies reached Chattanooga, and the spirits of the Army of the Cumberland rose in proportion.

General Bragg did not view this change in the programme favorably, and sent Longstreet to attack the forces guarding what General Grant called his "cracker line." But Longstreet was repulsed by General [John White] Geary, and did not repeat the attack.

On the 20th of November, re-enforcements under General [William Tecumseh] Sherman arrived, and taking advantage of this and the fact that Bragg had detached a portion of his force, Grant, who had been preparing to move upon the confederate position, issued the necessary orders.

Sherman was to attack the enemy on his right, and advance

to "the tunnel"; Hooker was directed to do the same on Bragg's left; and Thomas was expected to attack in the centre, as soon as the forces on the flanks became engaged.

On account of excessive rains and other unforeseen obstacles, the plan was slightly modified, and on the 23d, Thomas was directed to open the ball with [Gordon] Granger's corps (the divisions of [Thomas J.] Wood and Sheridan) and [John McC.] Palmer's corps (the divisions of [Absalom] Baird and [Richard W.] Johnson) on the right. After a brisk engagement, lasting all day, the enemy was driven back on his left for more than a mile.

On the 24th, Sherman's force crossed the Tennessee and attacked the enemy's right under cover of a mist. They reached the top of the ridge, but after two or three attempts to drive the Confederates from that point, were forced to intrench and take breath. On the same day, General Hooker had attacked Lookout Mountain, "fought the battle above the clouds," gained an important foothold on the eastern slope, and captured some 2,000 prisoners.

The morning of the next day, Nov. 25, dawned brightly upon the battle-field. At sunrise, Sherman made a vigorous attack upon the enemy's right flank and rear, threatening Bragg's communications and gaining some advantage; but the natural and artificial defences were so strong and the resistance so stout that,

after severe fighting, lasting nearly all day, the Union forces at this point of the line were barely holding their own. General Grant now ordered a diversion in Sherman's favor, by a charge of Thomas's troops in the centre and immediately in front of Orchard Knob. Hooker's operations on the right had not been so unobstructed as anticipated; and his troops had been delayed four precious hours in crossing Chattanooga Creek, as the enemy in retiring had burned the bridges.

General Grant says in this period of the fight: "Sheridan's and Wood's divisions had been lying under arms from early in the morning, ready to move the instant the signal was given. I directed Thomas to order the charge at once. The enemy was strongly intrenched on the crest of the ridge in front of us, and had a second line half-way down, and another at the base. Our men drove the troops in front of the lower line of rifle pits so rapidly, and followed them so closely, that rebel and Union troops went over the first line of works almost at the same time. Many rebels were captured and sent to the rear under the fire of their own friends half-way up the hill.[1] Without awaiting fur-

---

1. NOTE.—General Whipple (who was General Thomas's chief-of-staff) says that he was carrying an order to General Wood at this time, and met numbers of the enemy running toward him in a very headlong and demoralized manner, without their guns; they were making haste to get away from the fire of their own people higher up the hill, and sought safety behind the advancing Federals.

ther orders or stopping to re-form, on our troops went to the second line of works, over that and on for the crest. I watched their progress with intense interest. The fire along the rebel line was terrific; cannon and musket balls filled the air." General Howard says of this sight: "The enemy fly up the ridge without stopping to re-form. With no particular namable formation, in squads, with flags now drooping, now fallen, again uplifted, the men, with no more orders, followed by their officers move on up, up the ridge. Batteries upon the crest bear upon them and burst the shells over their heads, and cross-musketry fire from the rifle trenches on the heights kills some and wounds others, but our men do not stop until they have fully crowned the summit of this angry mountain and turned the enemy's guns to fire in another direction,—upon his own fragments." General Grant says of this moment: "General Thomas, with his staff, General Gordon Granger, commander of the corps making the assault, and myself and staff, occupied Orchard Knob, from which the entire field could be observed."

*This is the scene which the artist, M. de Thulstrup, has successfully depicted.*

In the group of three figures in the left foreground will be recognized the compact form of General Grant lifting his field-glass to his eye; on his left stands General Granger; while

the heroic proportions of General Thomas, then newly christened "Rock of Chicamauga," stand out boldly against the horizon. Near this historic trio may be seen a signal officer vainly endeavoring to communicate with General Sherman, for whose relief the attack immediately in front has been made. Farther in rear stand officers of the staff in attendance upon the principal commanders. To the right is the corps headquarters flag and color-guard with their horses.

The battle of Chattanooga was full of those incidents peculiar to war, but which are too often overshadowed by the important results of the operations of which they are not the least interesting part. The limited space available here permits but a passing allusion to one or two occurrences of this nature.

The signal for the charge of Sheridan's and Wood's divisions was the firing of six guns from Orchard Knob. The first gun was aimed at a point on the centre of the ridge believed to be Bragg's headquarters; it was afterwards learned that this shot blew up a Confederate caisson.

General Whipple was carrying an order from Orchard Knob. Just as the advancing line had carried the rifle-pits at the foot of the ridge, he encountered two men carrying a wounded officer of an Ohio regiment. [General William D.] Whipple, who wore the uniform of a brigadier-general, was

88

surprised at the salutation from the occupant of the stretcher, of "How are you, *Lieutenant?*" It proved to be a former private of Whipple's company in the Third Infantry of the Regular Army, who, while leading his brave volunteers up the ridge, had been hit in the leg.

General Howard relates a pathetic incident. After the last charge, four stout men carried a sergeant to the rear. They stopped to rest. E. P. Smith, then of the Christian Commission, drew near the stretcher, and speaking kindly, asked, "Where are you hurt, sergeant?" He answers, "Almost up, sir." "I mean, in what part are you injured?" He fixes his eye on the speaker, and answers again, "Almost up to the top." Just then Mr. Smith uncovers his arm, and sees the frightful shattering wound of the shell that struck him. "Yes," he says, turning his eye thither, "that's what did it. I was almost up: but for that I should have reached the top." The sergeant was bearing the flag when he was hit. He died with the fainter and fainter utterance of "Almost up," while his companions on the heights he almost reached were echoing the cheers of the triumph that he would have so much enjoyed.

General Sheridan with characteristic ardor had led his division in person, and says that, on arriving at the top of the hill on horseback, he was looking along the parapet to find a place to jump his horse over the works; some of the Confederates, unable to get away, thrust the buts [*sic*] of their muskets toward him in token of surrender. Suddenly, the general felt himself seized from behind, and nearly pulled off his horse. It proved to be one of his own colonels, who, thinking that his commander was needlessly exposing himself, adopted this unceremonious way to save his life.

By universal testimony, the completeness of the success at Missionary Ridge was due to the promptness with which Sheridan, without specific orders, pursued the enemy after the crest had been carried.

It has been estimated that the forces actually engaged numbered 45,000 Confederate and 55,000 Union soldiers; the advantage in position would be considered, however, as giving the Southern side superior numbers. Grant's casualties were 757 killed, 4,529 wounded, and 330 missing; total, 5,616. Bragg's loss was nearly 10,000 in all, of which number more than 6,000 were captured, together with 40 pieces of artillery and 7,000 small arms.

The battle of Chattanooga was one of the most important events of the year, which comprised in its history the great achievements of Vicksburg and Gettysburg.

# *Kenesaw Mountain*

## THE CHARGE OF LOGAN'S CORPS

After the battle of Murfreesboro, in 1863, Bragg's army fell back to Chattanooga. [Union General William S.] Rosecrans spent two months in recruiting; then pressing around the Confederates, he essayed to cut off their communication with Atlanta. Then followed the battles of Chickamauga and Chattanooga. Defeat and victory for the Union arms. During three November days in 1863, around Chattanooga, on Lookout, above the clouds, and along the rugged slopes of Missionary Ridge, the armies of the Cumberland and the Tennessee fought for the key to the heart of the Southern domain, and won it. Simultaneously with Grant's advance across the Rapidan to cope with Lee, Sher-

man's combined armies of the Cumberland, Tennessee, and the Ohio moved from Dalton to cope with [Confederate General Joseph E.] Johnston. Slowly but steadily, from one vantage point to another, Johnston retired until Atlanta was reached. That stronghold fell Sept.1; and in November, Sherman began his famous march to the sea.

In the series of engagements from Dalton to Atlanta was fought the battle of Kenesaw Mountain. Johnston's army occupied the mountain, its left wing extending across to Lost Mountain and its right wing resting on Pim Mountain. The Confederates at this time numbered about sixty thousand men, having been re-enforced, and their line extended a distance of about ten miles, of which General Sherman says, in his memoirs, "Too long, in my judgment, to be held successfully by his force." This became evident when the Union lines drew closer, and on the 15th of June, Pim Mountain was abandoned. The day previous, when the necessity for this move became apparent, Generals Johnston and [William J.] Hardee, and also General (Bishop) [Leonidas] Polk, rode to the summit of the hill to take a few of the surrounding country, in conspicuous view of both armies, probably silhouetted against the sky. The group attracted the attention of General Sherman. Thinking that it would be well to scatter them, and so break up the conference, he told General Howard to fire upon them. The gun was well sighted; an unexploded shell struck General Polk on the breast and killed him instantly. The next morning the Confederate right wing, under Hood, was forced back a little, and Hooker and Geary made a sharp attack upon the main line, under [Patrick R.] Cleburne, but were driven back, although Price Mountain was abandoned, and the next day (June 16th) the Confederates retired from Lost Mountain, the Federal batteries having gained command of their position. The Confederates fell back to a position about a mile west of the western end of Kenesaw Mountain, but were driven from here also, after some obstinate fighting. They then intrenched themselves in a position having for its key Kenesaw Mountain, and extending between that and the railroad to Marietta. The twin peaks, Big and Little Kenesaw, were occupied by batteries. Big Kenesaw afforded room on its summit for but a few guns, but Little Kenesaw—a commanding ridge extending perhaps a thousand feet before the precipitous descent at either end begins—formed a superb position for artillery. [Confederate] General [Samuel G.] French occupied this ridge with his division. The ascent to the ridge was difficult, and rendered hazardous by the Federal batteries on the neighboring heights, to whose fire it was completely exposed. General French, realizing the danger, waited until darkness spread its protecting cloak, and then dragged his guns to the summit up a back road by means of ropes, and on the morning of the 20th had twenty of them planted up on the mountain, protected by well-constructed works. From this mountain crest the Confederate guns poured upon the Federal troops below on the 22d and again on the 25th, and on both occasions met with a fierce reply from the Federal batteries. General Sherman brought to bear upon this position about one hundred and forty guns.

About fifty miles of this beautiful country, dotted with hills and crossed by ravines and picturesque valleys, were turned into a fort. The crests of the hills were occupied by artillery commanding the valleys at their base, and, in turn, commanded by higher hills, surmounted also by artillery. The ravines afforded roadways, sheltered by the hills, for any flank movements on the part of the troops. It was impossible in such a country as this for a force to prevent itself from being outflanked, if greatly outnumbered. This Sherman fully realized, and he began a series of flanking movements on his right, hoping to compel the enemy by counter-movements to extend its line until it became too attenuated for strength, and then to make an assault. He says: "I reasoned that if we could make a breach anywhere near the rebel centre and thrust in a strong head of column, that with one moiety of our army we could hold in check the corresponding wing of the enemy, and with the other sweep in flank and overwhelm the other half." All during the day and night of the 24th, flank movements were going on, and most of the time the sound of heavy cannonading filled the air, and during the night added a wild beauty to the scene, as flash succeeded flash in the darkness.

At last, on the 27th of June, 1864, a general and fierce assault was made by the Federals, which began the famous battle of Kenesaw Mountain. It was a sharp attack, lasting less than three hours, but taxing to their utmost the courage and energy of the Federal troops, and the fortitude and determination of John-

ston's army. Sherman's men again and again charged the enemy in a resolute but vain effort to gain the summit of the mountain; each time they were met by such a persistent and destructive fire from French's batteries, on the crest of the hills, that their attempts resulted only in terrible loss of life. Twice the Union men seemed almost to have gained the parapet, but were swept back by an awful shower of fire poured upon them from above. General [Charles G.] Harker, who led one of these desperate assaults, was shot down almost at the parapet, and General [Daniel] McCook was severely wounded. In the very hot test of the battle the men were distinguishing themselves by special feats of personal bravery. A shrapnel shell with a burning fuse, hurled from one of Sherman's guns, fell among a group of men in a ditch. A stampede began, but before the explosion came, a gallant Georgia sergeant leaped forward, and seizing the burning projectile, hurled it over the intrenchment. Two or three hand-to-hand contests for colors occurred during Harker's dash upon [Confederate General Benjamin Franklin] Cheatham's troops. A Union flag was planted upon the top of the works; instantly it was seized by a Confederate captain, and for a few minutes a desperate struggle ensued with the color-bearer; then the captain fell; in a second, twenty rifles flashed out against the brave Union man, and, riddled with balls, he dropped to the ground, clasping firmly the colors he had so bravely struggled to retain. Immediately the flag was captured. Not far from this spot a Confederate sergeant made a bold dash over the works, and seizing a Union flag, returned with it in triumph. General Hardee afterwards presented the flag to him in recognition of his bravery.

While this was going on around the western end of Kenesaw Mountain, General [John A.] Logan, with three brigades formed in three lines, and supported by Blair and Dodge, was making a desperate attack upon the Confederate left wing, which stretched from the east end of the mountain across the railroad that curved around its base, and past the village of Elizabeth to the hills beyond. The Twelfth Louisiana Regiment occupied rifle pits, a long line of which had been made about six hundred yards in front of the main line of intrenchments. On came the Federal forces to within twenty-five paces of the enemy, facing all the time a constant and sharp fusillade. Then with all haste the Louisianians retired to their line of battle. Logan's men pushed on till they encountered Featherstone's troops, who received them with a volley of musketry so destructive and fierce that they were compelled to halt. From the mountain shot and shell fell like hail, making great gaps in the columns that held their ground so bravely. They

took position in the forest, and under its protection returned steadily the enemy's furious fire. The Confederate artillery kept up its appalling fire, but the brave Union men were loath to retreat, though their ranks were fast melting away. Any advance under such a fire was impossible. For an hour they held their ground. Hundreds of men fell, and seven regiments lost their commanding officers. Some of these had fallen within twenty feet of the Confederate works. At last, Logan, feeling that a continuation of the slaughter was useless, withdrew his men to the rifle pits that they had previously captured from the Louisiana troops. Farther along the line, Wheeler and Quarles were resisting a fierce and impetuous assault from the Federals, and all along the mountain desperate charges were made that in every instance met with an effective artillery rebuke from the batteries which French had placed on its crest. Fierce and hot was the struggle. Bravely fought the Union men, while thousands of their number were slain. During a portion of the action the dry leaves and underbrush began to burn, ignited by bursting shells. Hundreds of wounded men lay on the ground now assailed by the new and even greater horror of being burned alive. The Confederates saw this appalling situation, and instantly the order was given to cease firing. The Confederate commander notified the Federals that as an act of common humanity further battle would be suspended until the wounded could be carried beyond the range of the flames. Gladly was this humane offer accepted, and with all speed the poor fellows, many of them dying, were carried to some spot where at least they would not be burned. Turning from this act of humanity, they renewed the combat with increased zeal, but without success. The Federal troops were obliged to withdraw from all the points of assault. For three hours the struggle had lasted, in which were engaged 100,000 men. The superiority in numbers of the Union force was more than balanced by the advantage of the position held by the Confederates.

A great move of the campaign had failed. Johnston's army still held Kenesaw Mountain, which Sherman called "the key to the whole country," but Sherman lost no time in mourning over the defeat. With characteristic energy he began at once a strong movement around the mountain down the valley of Olley's Creek, with the view of reaching the railroad below Marietta by a long circuit. Johnston found the position he had fought so well to hold must after all be resigned, or else his communications with Atlanta would be cut off; so on the 1st and 2d of July the Confederate lines were withdrawn from Kenesaw and Marietta, and the difficult work of lowering the batteries from the mountain was carried on under cover of the night. The Confederates fell back to a new position, well prepared and strongly intrenched. Then succeeded the sharp fight at Buff's Station and Smyrna, followed on the 20th of July, after Johnston had been succeeded in the command by Hood, by the battle of Peach Tree Creek, and on the 22d by a fierce battle, in which General [James B.] McPherson of the Federal Army and General [William H. T.] Walker of the Confederates lost their lives. Again, on the 28th, occurred the battle of Ezra Church. In all of these encounters the Confederates suffered severe losses, and lost ground. A month later Atlanta was evacuated, and Sherman passed through it on his way to the sea.

# HOLDING THE PASS AT

## *Allatoona*

The pass of Allatoona, the scene of General John M. Corse's stubborn fight to "hold the fort," in October, 1864, is a narrow railroad cut through the Allatoona range of mountains. The actual field of battle was the line of heights, cut into almost equal eastern and western halves by the beginning of the pass. Through this opening rises in the north the Allatoona Mountain, where the signals were received from Sherman at Kenesaw to "hold fast," for "I am coming." Sherman had penetrated the Southern Confederacy to Atlanta, and was bringing his supplies three hundred and thirty-six miles by rail from Louisville, when Hood turned on his lines, and got between him and Allatoona in the opening days of October.

In the village, at the foot of the heights, were 2,700,000 rations, and Colonel Tourtellotte, the commander, had only about six hundred fighting men to defend them. On the 4th, Sherman sent word to Corse, who was in Rome, forty miles to the northwest, to move his command to Allatoona, and hold it. General Corse, though the youngest general in the army, was one in whom Sherman most implicitly trusted, and one of the best qualified for the severe task before him. He received his orders at about eight o'clock on the evening of the 4th, and at once ordered the First Brigade to prepare to move. Only one locomotive and twenty cars were available, and they had to be unloaded of hard-tack, and brought from Kingston,

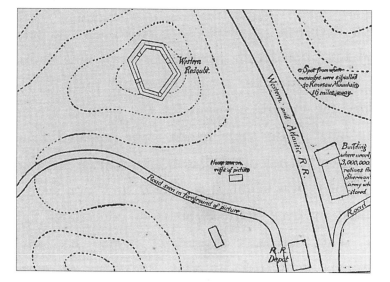

twenty miles away. Spreading rails, washouts, and derailments delayed the journey, so that it was nearly one o'clock in the morning of the 5th when about one thousand fighting men were added to the meagre garrison of the heights.

The pickets had already been driven in, and brisk firing showed that the enemy had invested the place in force. Corse, accompanied by Colonel Richard Rowett, of Illinois, made the circuit of the lines in the darkness, and prepared his plans for the day. Only a little foot-bridge joined the heights on either side of the railroad cut, and it was necessary to divide the little garrison in advance with careful regard to the contingencies of action. When morning came, the Confederate attack was made from all sides. From Myrick's Hill, about half a mile to the south, a battery of thirteen guns dropped shell into the Federal lines. On the west, [William H.] Young's famous brigade of Texans and [Francis M.] Cockrell's Missouri brigade marched up the highway, while Sears's brigade attacked from the north. The total Confederate force, by their own official reports, was 5,600 men. The 1,600 Union troops were carefully disposed on the heights, the larger number to the west, protected by some light earthworks, with two pieces of artillery on each side of the cut.

When French, the Confederate commander, had made his dispositions, he sent in a curt message to Corse to surrender, "to avoid a needless effusion of blood," and gave him five minutes to consider it. In less than the time allowed the young Federal commander had dictated his reply, that he was prepared for the "needless effusion of blood" whenever it was agreeable to the enemy. At once the attack began on all sides. While the artillery shelled the Federal lines, daring individual soldiers attempted to creep up to the stores to set them on fire, and one was found after the battle within thirty yards, prone upon the ground with an extinguished torch in his hand. On the west, where Corse commanded in person, Cockrell and Young forced their way up the road over the first weak defences, and though suffering terrible losses, reached close to the last redoubt on the crest of the height. At about one o'clock, a bullet ploughed across General Corse's cheek, cutting through his cheek and ear, and rendering him insensible. He regained consciousness at about 1:45, to hear Colonel Richard Rowett, who was in command, give the order to "cease firing." Thinking at the moment that it meant surrender, he sharply countermanded the order, and with bandaged, bleeding head moved from point to point, inspiring the defence.

Meantime, on the eastern height, Colonel Tourtellotte manfully held his ground, and by catching a part of the attacking column of Sears between the converging fire of two lines of earthworks, made several hundred prisoners. But the brunt of the attack came on the little garrison of the western heights. Cockrell's brigade was nearly exterminated, but Young's fierce Texans drove the little Northern force from point to point, closer to the feeble earthworks. Towards the middle of the afternoon, when the Federal guns had been silenced for want of ammunition, a strong Confederate column of attack was observed forming in a ravine to the northwest. It was to be the charge of the last reserves, like that of the Imperial Guard at Waterloo, and Corse met it with more than the spirit of " the Iron Duke," for he was without ammunition, bleeding with wounds, and with no hope of prompt re-enforcement. Minie-balls, wrapped in strips of blanket, were forced into the little field-piece, and the men loaded their smoking muskets from their fast diminishing hoard of bullets. On came the Confederates, officers leading, flags flying, and soldiers shouting the frightful "rebel yell." When at the distance of two hundred yards from the redoubt, the guns of the Federals spoke, and the rebel lines broke in demoralizing, panic-stricken defeat.

Then Corse uttered something like Wellington's order, "Up, guards, and at them!" and the remnant of his little garrison leaped over the breastworks, charged with bayonets and clubbed muskets, and drove the Confederates far down the hill. It is this scene which our artist depicts.

98

The battle was won, and Corse was able to telegraph to Sherman, "I am short a cheekbone and an ear, but am able to whip all hell yet!" He added, with pathetic truthfulness, "My losses are very heavy." The little redoubt was encumbered by the dead. They had to be moved to make way for the gun, when it was put in position for its last discharge. Corse's losses, out of about 1,600 fighting men, were 142 killed, 352 wounded, and 212 missing; the missing, however, included a detachment of about 90 men captured in a block-house at Allatoona Creek, who were not in the battle at the pass. The Confederate loss was estimated by General Young, who was taken prisoner, at 2,000.

Sherman had heard the distant firing all day, and when it ceased he feared that Allatoona had fallen. Had the Confederate commander been able to form his men for another attack, he would probably have carried the Federal position, for the guns of the men were bursting in their hands from repeated firing; only a few rounds of small-arm ammunition remained, the artillery was silent, and officers and men were exhausted by over fourteen hours of continuous fighting. The "needless effusion of blood" had saved Allatoona, protected its vast quantities of stores, foiled Hood's plans, and made possible the "march to the sea." General Sherman was so pleased with the defence that he made it the subject of a special order, praising General Corse, his officers and men, and pointing out that it illustrated "the most important principle in war, that fortified posts should be defended to the last, regardless of the relative numbers of the party attacking and attacked."

# SIEGE OF

## *Atlanta*

On March 18, 1864, General Sherman was appointed in command of the Military Division of the Mississippi, which embraced the departments of the Ohio, Cumberland, Tennessee, and Arkansas. General Grant had been called East at this time as commander-in-chief of all the armies in the field, and was personally to direct the movements of the Army of the Potomac.

Sherman was to advance against Johnston's army, and for which Atlanta had similar importance to that which the capital of Virginia had for Lee. General Sherman says of the campaign: "Neither Atlanta, nor Augusta, nor Savannah was the objective, but the 'army of Jos. Johnston,' go where it might."

After the battle of Chattanooga, General Bragg had been removed from command of the Army of Northern Georgia, and that army, now under command of General Jos. Johnston, was strongly fortified at Dalton. On the 6th of May the Federal forces advanced from Chattanooga against this point, which a few days later was evacuated by the Confederates. Then followed a series of hard-fought battles, while slowly retreating over mountains and across rivers, contending every point until the two armies confronted each other before Atlanta, in the early days of July. On the 17th of the month a general movement was begun against that city.

Atlanta was known as the "Gate City of the South." It was

the centre of an important railroad system, was full of foundries, arsenals, and machine shops, the capture of which would be an irreparable loss to the Confederacy. The city was situated on a high plateau, from which the streams descend in all directions, making it, therefore, a strong defensive point.

On July 22, a severe engagement took place along the lines held by the Army of the Tennessee, which resulted in driving the enemy within the entrenchments proper of the city, which were in a general circle, with a radius of one and a half miles. During the month the Confederate authorities of Richmond removed General Johnston from command, and in his stead had appointed General J.B. Hood.

General Sherman, in his memoirs, says: "The month of August opened hot and sultry, but our position before Atlanta was healthy, with ample supply of wood, water, and provisions. The troops had become habituated to the slow and steady progress of the siege; the skirmish lines were held close up to the enemy, were covered by rifle trenches or logs, and kept up a continuous clatter of musketry. The main lines were held farther back, adapted to the shape of the ground, with muskets loaded for instant use. The field batteries were in select positions, covered by handsome parapets, and occasional shots from them gave life and animation to the scene. The men loi-tered about the trenches carelessly, or busied themselves in constructing ingenious huts out of the abundant timber, and seemed as snug, comfortable, and happy as though they were at home. General [John M.] Schofield was on the extreme left, Thomas in the centre, and Howard on the right."

On Aug. 7, Sherman telegraphed General Halleck: ". . . We keep hammering away all the time, and there is no peace inside or outside of Atlanta. . . . I have sent back to Chattanooga for two thirty-pound Parrotts, with which we can pick out almost any house in Atlanta. I am too impatient for a siege, and don't know but this is as good a place to fight it out on as farther inland. One thing is certain, whether we get inside of Atlanta or not, it will be a used-up community when we are done with it."

During the entire month, a general artillery fire was maintained, and engagements by the infantry columns, along some portion of the long lines which nearly encircled the city, were frequent, as they gradually closed in, capturing the various defences and fortified positions. Cavalry columns, under the dashing [Judson] Kilpatrick, had made the complete circuit around Atlanta, tearing up railroads and inflicting other damage.

On the morning of Aug. 31, a general movement was begun to destroy the remaining railroad communication to the city.

Schofield's troops reached it near Rough and Ready, and those of General Thomas, near Jonesboro' General Sherman says:

> "All hands were kept busy tearing up the railroad, and it was not until toward eveneing of the first day of September that the Fourteenth Corps (Davis) closed down on the north front of Jonesboro', connecting on his right with Howard, and his left reaching the railroad along which General [David S.] Stanley was moving, followed by Schofield. General [Jefferson Columbus] Davis formed his divisions in line about 4 P.M., swept forward over some old cotton fields in full view, and went over the rebel parapet handsomely, capturing the whole of Govan's brigade, with two field batteries of ten guns. Being on the spot, I checked Davis's movement, and ordered General Howard to send two divisions of the Seventeenth Corps (Blair) round by his right rear, to get below Jonesboro', and to reach the railroad, so as to cut off retreat in that direction."

During the night of Sept. 1, ominous sounds of heavy explosions were heard in the direction of the city, and in the early morning General [Henry W.] Slocum moved rapidly forward with the Twentieth Corps, and entered Atlanta unopposed. The news was signalled and sent by courier to the different divisions of the army, and the cheers of the men went up in grand chorus over the great victory. "Atlanta is ours and fairly won," telegraphed General Sherman to Washington, and from the capital and Northern cities were returned the heartiest congratulations over the opportune victory. The Northern States, then in the midst of a Presidential campaign, were fighting "the enemy in the rear." A political party had in its platform declared the war a failure; advocated that the South be allowed to secede and establish a separate government, with slavery as her corner-stone. The success of the national forces was, therefore, at that time, a political necessity, and the brilliant success of Sherman's army, "way down in Dixie," carried forward the impending campaign to the triumphant re-election of President Lincoln.

Hood, with his army, had retreated a short distance from Atlanta, and fortified. Sherman held the city and its environs, and had decided to give his army a short period of rest, and prepare for the next movement in the campaign. From the city all non-combatants, men, women, and children, were to be removed, each given the choice of direction, and, with their household goods, were transported north, or south to the enemy's lines at the neutral camp established at Rough and Ready.

During the latter part of September, General Hood began a movement toward the rear of the Union Army, to cut off communication with Nashville, the base of supplies, by destroying

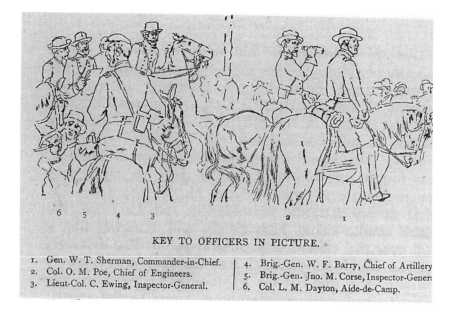

KEY TO OFFICERS IN PICTURE.

1. Gen. W. T. Sherman, Commander-in-Chief.
2. Col. O. M. Poe, Chief of Engineers.
3. Lieut-Col. C. Ewing, Inspector-General.
4. Brig.-Gen. W. F. Barry, Chief of Artillery
5. Brig.-Gen. Jno. M. Corse, Inspector-Gener:
6. Col. L. M. Dayton, Aide-de-Camp.

the railroad leading from Atlanta to that city. The fortified stations of Allatoona and Resaca were attacked without success, but striking the railroad at different points interrupted telegraphic communication, tore up tracks, and destroyed bridges. Hood's movements soon convinced Sherman that his object was to avoid battle and to draw him away from the position that he had gained; therefore to General Thomas was assigned the task of holding Hood in check, while the remainder of the army returned to Atlanta, presenting the strange event of two hostile armies marching in opposite directions, each believing that their movements would result in a conclusive result in the history of the war.

The Union Army occupied Atlanta until the first of November, when that portion of the city which could be made available to the enemy for furnishing the sinews of war was destroyed by fire. On the 12th, all railroad and telegraph communication with the rear was broken, and the army, separated from friends, dependent upon its own resources, began preparations for the famous "March to the Sea."

General Sherman, in his memoirs, says:

"About 7 A.M. of Nov. 16, we rode out of Atlanta by the Decatur road, filled by the marching troops and wagons of the Fourteenth Corps; and reaching the hill just outside of the old rebel works, we naturally paused to look back upon the scenes of our past battles. We stood upon the very ground whereon was fought the bloody battle of July 22, and could see the copse of wood where McPherson fell. Behind us lay Atlanta, smouldering and in ruins, the black smoke rising high in air, and hanging like a pall over the ruined city. Away off in the distance on the McDonough road, was the rear of Howard's column, the gun barrels glistening in the sun, the white-topped wagons stretching away to the south; and right behind us, the Fourteenth Corps, marching steadily and rapidly, with cheery look and steady pace, that made light of the thousand miles that lay between us and Richmond.

"Then we turned our horses' heads to the east. Atlanta was soon lost behind the screen of trees, and became a thing of the past. Around it clings many thoughts of desperate battle, of hope and fear, that now seem like the memory of a dream. The day was extremely beautiful, clear sunlight, and bracing air, and an unusual feeling of exhilaration seemed to pervade all minds,—a feeling of something to come, vague and undefined, still full of venture and intense interest."

103

# Siege of Vicksburg

## ASSAULT ON FORT HILL

After the various abortive attempts to either capture or invest Vicksburg from above, General Grant transferred the bulk of his army to Bruinsburg, six miles below Grand Gulf, and within twenty days had met and defeated the enemy at Port Gibson, Raymond, Jackson, Champion's Hill, and Big Black River; had killed, wounded and captured about thirteen thousand men; taken sixty-one pieces of field artillery and twenty-seven heavy cannon; opened communication with the National fleet at the mouth of the Yazoo, and driven [John C.] Pemberton into the defences of the great Confederate stronghold, from whence his army of thirty-one thousand men were to issue only as paroled prisoners of war.

The battle of Champion's Hill not only destroyed the possibility of a junction of the forces of Pemberton and Johns[t]on, but ended in the complete rout and demoralization of Pemberton's army, so that when they reached the Big Black River, where a position of great natural strength had been skilfully fortified, but slight resistance was made to the magnificent charge of [Michael K.] Lawler's brigade of [Eugene A.] Carr's division, and a panic ensued which ended most disastrously to the enemy. A wild scramble followed for the river, but those on the western bank caught the infection and set fire to the bridge before one half of their comrades were across, and seventeen hundred and fifty-two prisoners were captured, among whom was an East Tennessee brigade, which did not fire a shot, they having no heart in the war, and desiring to surrender and go home.

On the 18th of May, 1863, Grant arrived in the rear of Vicksburg, and, relying upon the demoralized condition of the enemy and upon the prowess of his own victorious army, he gave orders to his corps commanders to push forward carefully on the next day, "and gain positions as close as possible to the enemy's works, until two o'clock P.M. At that hour, they will fire three volleys of artillery from all the pieces in position. This will be the signal for a general charge along the whole line." The result of the assault was unsuccessful, beyond that of securing advanced positions for the National lines and accompanying artillery.

The ground upon which the city of Vicksburg stands was once a plateau some four or five miles long and about two miles wide, varying from two to three hundred feet above the river. The soil is fine, hard clay, which has been traversed by the rains into deep gullies and ravines, with sides nearly vertical, upon which had grown in many places an impenetrable and luxuriant mass of foliage. On the north of the town the line of defences ran to the eastward from the river about two miles, crowning a ridge between two ravines, then turned to the

southward, conforming to the crest of another dividing ridge, crossed transverse ravines and enclosed the city, striking the river on the south at Hall's Ferry. The defences consisted of a series of detached works from seventy-five to one hundred yards apart, and connected by breastworks. In front of the detached works were deep ditches, but the ravines formed all but impassable barriers in front of most of the connecting entrenchments. Along the whole line trees were felled, and the entangled branches formed obstacles which were impassable for bodies of troops. At the point where the carriage road from Jackson reached the defensive line stood a large fort, which for some reason became known within the Union lines as Fort Hill. Much confusion has been caused by the fact that on the extreme left of the Confederate line, on the north of the city, was another large work which had long been known by the same name, and it is generally to this fort that reference is made in reports wherein Fort Hill is named. It is to the fort on the Jackson road that this article primarily relates, as it is one of the assaults upon this formidable work which has been chosen by M. de Thulstrup for his picture, which is known in the series as "The Siege of Vicksburg; Assault on Fort Hill."

The Jackson road approached the defensive line from the east along a ridge which crossed nearly at right angles a ravine which ran along in front of the Confederate works at this point, and it was to command the approach from the Jackson road that this strong fort was erected. The ground upon which it was situated was high, and it overlooked almost the entire Union lines.

Notwithstanding the failure of the assault on the 19th of May, General Grant still believed that he could, from the advanced positions then attained, successfully storm the Confederate works, and while the loss of life would necessarily be large, it would be less than during a protracted siege. Another important consideration was that General Joseph E. Johnston was collecting a large force at Canton for the purpose of attacking him in the rear, whereby he might, with the co-operation of Pemberton, raise the siege.

On the 21st, Grant issued orders for a general assault along the line at ten o'clock A.M. on the following day, and directed corps commanders to carefully examine all approaches to the enemy's works, to place all available artillery in position, and advance their skirmishers as far as possible. On the same day he wrote Admiral [David Dixon] Porter: "I expect to assault the city at ten A.M. to-morrow. I would request that you send up the gun-boats below the city, and shell the rebel entrenchments until that hour, and for thirty minutes thereafter. If the mortars could all be sent down to near the point on the Louisiana shore, and throw in shells during the night, it would materially aid me."

Porter complied with this request, and six mortars were kept throwing their huge shells into the city all night, while three gun-boats shelled the water batteries. At three o'clock in the morning the artillery surrounding the city was opened. Sharp-shooters advantageously placed fired incessantly, and a pandemonium of destruction was poured upon the besieged and continued until the moment of the assault, which enabled the troops to form without molestation.

At the appointed time a most heroic assault was made along the entire line, which resulted in a complete repulse. Grant became satisfied that success was impossible, when he received a despatch from [General John A.] McClernand, who commanded on his extreme left: "We are hotly engaged with the enemy. We have part possession of two forts, and the stars and stripes are floating over them. A vigorous push ought to be made all along the line." The result of this misleading dispatch was a second fruitless assault, which doubled the number of killed and wounded on the Union side, and accomplished nothing beyond. Union flags were planted upon the works at several places, but no troops could gain a lodgment to protect them, while the fierce and deadly fire of the Federal sharp-shooters rendered futile all attempts on the part of the enemy to capture them. It was demonstrated that whatever demoralization existed in Pemberton's army when it reached Vicksburg, there was none now. His men fought with all the old valor of Shiloh and Corinth, and against their all but impregnable defences a siege was the only resource left for success.

Grant now made every preparation to starve the besieged into surrender. Batteries were placed in advantageous positions, and connected by lines of parapet, rifle-trench, and covered way; permanent camps were formed, which, when occasion required, were also connected by sheltered passageways. Logan's division of McPherson's corps occupied the line crossing the Jackson road, and a sap was constructed along this road toward the large fort which commanded the position. As the sap approached the fort it was covered by gabions made from cane, which grew in abundance near. When within seventy-five feet of the enemy's works, ditches were dug at right angles with the sap, and occupied by troops, who gradually advanced until the men on both sides were able to converse and exchange rations by throwing them over the intervening salient.

From the head of the sap before mentioned a mine was driven directly under the fort, more than thirty feet below the surface. Three different branch mines were constructed, and twenty-seven hundred pounds of powder placed in them. They were tamped with cross-timbers and sand bags; fuses were arranged so as to explode at the same instant. The troops selected for the charge into the crater were from General M.D. Leggett's brigade of Logan's division, which consisted of the 20th, 30th, 31st, 45th, and 124th Illinois Infantry. The storming party consisted of two hundred men under the immediate command of General Leggett, while the balance of the brigade was under arms a short distance to the rear.

At about half past three on the afternoon of the 25th of June the torch was applied, and the great fort was lifted in the air and scattered in all directions. While the air was yet dark with the dust, *débris*, and smoke, General Leggett led his command into the crater, when he was met by a maddened foe, and a most desperate encounter ensued, which M. de Thulstrup has graphically illustrated. General Leggett was severely wounded almost at the moment of entering the crater, but he refused to be removed to the hospital, and was carried back a few paces to his trenches, where he remained, giving orders and receiving reports until the struggle ended.

The crater was cone-shaped, and the storming party was thus exposed to loaded shells and grenades thrown into their midst by hand with deadly effect. Such of the shells and grenades as did not explode were caught by the men and thrown back, causing havoc in the ranks of the Confederates. The Union troops had no grenades, but took instead shells, cut the fuse and threw them over to the foe. Finally, the enemy brought a piece of artillery close to the outer wall of the crater, and fired through the loose earth, stone, and timbers. The blaze from the gun would often reach and badly burn some of Leggett's men. This gun was finally dismounted and disabled by the large shells thrown by hand. An officer of General Logan's staff was cutting the fuses of shells, igniting and tossing them over the wall, when one exploded in his hands. Said an eye-witness: "I was standing near, and saw that the fuse was too short, and that it must explode. I threw myself upon my back, and in an instant came the report and we were enveloped in the smoke. When it cleared away I expected to see his mangled remains, but to my surprise he was apparently uninjured, and was coolly reaching for another shell." The contest was often a hand-to-hand struggle. The men would grapple and struggle fiercely for the mastery, but in such encounters the Union men were finally successful, as their foe had become enfeebled from insufficient food and long service in the trenches.

The struggle continued through the weary night and a part of the day following. The 56th Illinois Infantry led by Colonel Green B. Raum, was sent to hold the crater on the 26th, but having exhausted their ammunition, a supply of the wrong calibre was sent, which resulted in their defeat. At the time of the explosion a few Confederates were blown within the Union lines, one or two of whom came down alive. One negro came over and fell head first in a bank of loose sand in the rear of where the storming party was standing. He was pulled out and soon recovered. When asked how high he went, he answered, "Do' 'no', Massa; spec about tree miles; as I was coming down I met Massa goin' up, and he didn't 'no' how high we was."

# Battle of Shiloh

## "THE HORNETS' NEST"

T he success of the national forces at [Forts] Donelson and Henry, which immediately preceded the battle of Shiloh, had a most important bearing upon that conflict. General Grant, in his "Memoirs," says: "Up to the battle of Shiloh, I, as well as thousands of other citizens, believed that the Rebellion would collapse suddenly and soon, if a decisive victory could be gained over any of its armies. Donelson and Henry were such victories."

The Confederates, on the contrary, were rendered more determined by defeat. Delusive hopes had been raised by incompetent generals, and when the knowledge of the extent of the disaster which had compelled the abandonment of their defensive line, extending from Columbus to Bowling Green, became general, there was a savage resolve to crush and destroy Grant before he could accumulate a force sufficient to capture or compel the evacuation of that most important strategic point, Corinth.

When General Grant, after a short suspension by [General Henry W.] Halleck, resumed the command of his army on the 17th of March, 1862, he found the divisions of Sherman and [Stephen A.] Hurlburt at Pittsburg Landing on the west side of the Tennessee River; that of Lew Wallace was at Crump's Landing on the same side of the river, about five miles above, where he had been stationed by General C. F. Smith to protect the supplies and transports at that point. The division of C. F. Smith, subsequently commanded by General W. H. L. Wallace, was at Savannah, on the east side of the river, about nine miles distant.

Immediately on Grant's arrival, he issued orders for the removal of Smith's and McClernand's divisions to Pittsburg Landing, and General Prentiss having reported for duty was assigned to a new division organized of raw troops.

The forces at Pittsburg Landing, as well as Lew Wallace's division at Crump's Landing, had been so placed by order of General C. F. Smith, as a convenient point for the advance upon Corinth. As the divisions arrived, they took positions with a view to good camp and drill grounds rather than to defence against a probable attack. The flanks were protected by Owl and Snake Creeks, the ground was heavily timbered, with occasional open fields, and traversed by deep ravines. Had a continuous line been formed from Owl to Snake Creek, and earth-works thrown up as would have been done at a later period of the war by the men, even without orders, the army would have been impregnable against an attack from any force which could have been collected by Johnston until the arrival of [General Don Carlos] Buel[l] who was marching to Savannah with an army of forty thousand men. But at that time nei-

ther generals nor their commands were schooled in the art of war, and a new and terrible lesson was learned at a terrific cost.

On Sunday morning, April 6, 1862, the position of General Grant's forces was as follows: On the extreme right, resting near Owl Creek, was Sherman's division, consisting of McDowell's, Buckland's, and Hildebrand's brigades; McDowell's fronting towards the southwest, Buckland and Hildebrand facing south, with Shiloh Church to the rear and about midway of the space between Buckland's left and Hildebrand's right. The 53d Ohio Infantry were camped, however, about two hundred yards distant from the balance of Hildebrand's brigade, and across a ravine, the position having been selected for the purpose of enclosing within the brigade line a fine spring.

To the left, and more than half a mile to the front was Prentiss's division, consisting of new troops, entirely without drill or knowledge of field manœuvres. The distance between Sherman and Prentiss was largely increased and the latter formed his line of battle at six o'clock on Sunday morning. Stuart's brigade of Sherman's division, about three quarters of a mile to the left, formed the extreme left of Grant's forces. Rather more than a mile to the rear of Prentiss, was camped the division of Hurlburt, while McClernand lay half a mile to the rear of Sherman. About two miles from the front, to the right and

110

rear of Hurlburt, was the division of C. F. Smith, commanded by W. H. L. Wallace, General Smith being fatally ill.

It is necessary that the disposition of General Grant's forces should be borne in mind, in order that a correct understanding may be had of the battle which followed. The total available Union forces, as reported on the morning of the first day's fight, was thirty-three thousand men, but General Grant says, "Excluding the troops who fled panic-stricken before they had fired a shot, there was not a time during the 6th when we had more than twenty-five thousand men in line."

Johnston's effective force at the opening of the battle was reported by [Confederate General P. G. T.] Beauregard at 40,955 men, although General Grant claims that this is an understatement according to the method of enumeration used with the National forces, as at the South every man enlisted as a musician or detailed as a guard or nurse, including all commissioned officers, were excluded, while on the Union side everybody in the field under government pay was counted.

There had been signs of unusual activity on the part of the enemy several days before. Hostile squadrons of cavalry were seen hovering in the woods beyond the picket lines of Sherman and Prentiss. Reconnoitring parties were sent to the front, and severe skirmishing followed with the enemy's cavalry. Every one

in the two advanced divisions was on the alert, and Prentiss sent out three companies of the 25th Missouri at three o'clock Sunday morning, to reconnoitre, and moving to the southwest they struck the enemy's pickets in front of Sherman's division at fourteen minutes past five o'clock. Prentiss moved his division to a point in advance of his camps, and consequently received the first shock of battle, but as none of his men had heard a hostile shot until their arrival a few days before, they were soon driven back and a new line was formed inside the camps. When the enemy struck the left brigade of Sherman's division there was wavering, and soon after a stampede. The 53d Ohio being detached somewhat from Hildebrand's brigade, fired a couple of volleys and then received an order from its colonel to fall back and save themselves. As a result, the regiment fled in confusion behind a brigade of McClernand which had been sent to its support. The lieutenant-colonel and adjutant soon rallied the men, and they returned to the position to be once more stampeded by the cowardly colonel who reappeared and again gave the order to retreat. This ended the regimental organization for the day, although detachments joined other commands and fought bravely to the end.

Buckland on Hildebrand's right was attacked with the utmost fury by Cleburne's brigade of six regiments and two batteries of artillery, but gallantly held his ground and repulsed charge after charge until Cleburne lost more than one third of his brigade, killed and wounded, the 6th Mississippi having left three hundred, out of a total of four hundred and twenty-five, dead and wounded on the field.

The Confederates were quick to perceive the great gaps in the Federal lines, and poured through regiments and brigades, striking their enemy in the rear and flank, compelling changes of front to new positions of defence. The forces sent by McClernand to stem the tide passing between Sherman and Prentiss were flanked, defeated and driven back, and at ten o'clock Sherman took a new position to the rear along the Purdy road. McClernand's other brigades having taken position on the left of his third, being flanked by the overreaching lines of the enemy, after a sharp fight fell back and joined on Sherman's left and across the Corinth road, facing south. There was an interval between McClernand's left and the right of W. L. Wallace, whose division was at that time formed nearly at right angles with that of McClernand and facing west. Here McClernand stood his ground until late in the afternoon, resisting successfully most desperate attacks, at one time driving the enemy nearly half a mile to the rear. With his flanks unprotected he was forced back towards the northeast,

and in the afternoon re-formed his left so as to face the west. At ten o'clock W. H. L. Wallace came into action, placing Tuttle's brigade on Prentiss's right and that of Sweeney to the right of Tuttle. McArthur went with two regiments to the support of Stuart in his isolated position on the extreme left of the Union line. His other regiments having been detached for other purposes, it left Wallace with but two brigades of his own division.

On the left of Wallace was the remains of Prentiss's division, and still farther to the left was Hurlburt. Prentiss's line extended along an old sunken, abandoned road, running a little to the north of west. Hickenlooper's battery—or rather the four remaining guns, two having been captured—was placed on the right of the Corinth road nearly at its intersection with the old road above named, and still farther to the right on the same road was Munch's battery. General Grant gave Prentiss orders to hold his position at all hazards. He obeyed the order and stood the repeated assaults of the enemy.

In front of this position, upon which so largely depended the safety of the Union Army, the most desperate assaults were made, and this scene of heroic encounter has been selected by M. de Thulstrup for his spirited picture. The officer facing the spectator, giving directions to one of his artillerymen whom he has despatched for more ammunition, is Captain Hicken-looper, who fought his battery so magnificently; and to the right of the picture, seated upon his horse, giving orders to an officer of the 8th Iowa, is General Prentiss. The troops engaged at this point, and which come within the range of vision, are the 8th Iowa, Colonel Geddes; 12th Iowa, Colonel Wood; and 14th Iowa, Colonel Shaw; while Munch's and Welker's batteries were stationed at proper intervals along the line.

The actual encounter is best described by Colonel Wm. Preston Johnston in the Life of his father, from which we quote:—

"And now both armies were in the tumult of mortal endeavor. The Confederate assaults were made by rapid and often unconnected charges along the line. They were repeatedly checked, and often repulsed, by the stubborn resistance of the assailed. Sometimes counter-charges drove them back for a short distance; but whether in assault or recoil, both sides saw their bravest soldiers fall in frightful numbers. Over the blue-clad lines of the Federal troops floated the 'Stars and Stripes,' endeared to them by the traditions of three quarters of a century. The Confederates came out in motley garb, varying from favorite gray and domestic 'butternut,' to the blue of certain Lousiana regiments, which paid so dearly the penalty of doubtful colors. Over them were flags and pennons, as various as their uniforms.

"Polk and Bragg, meeting about half past ten o'clock, agreed that Polk should direct the left centre, where part of his corps were grouped, and that Bragg should take command of his right. Bragg says:—

"'Here we met the most obstinate resistance of the day, the enemy being strongly posted with infantry and artillery on an eminence behind a dense thicket. [Thomas C.] Hindman's command was gallantly led to the attack, but recoiled under a murderous fire.'

"Hindman himself was severely wounded by the explosion of a shell, and borne from the field. A.P. Stewart then took command of Hindman's brigade with his own.

"This position of the Federals was occupied by Wallace's division, and perhaps by the remains of Prentiss's and other commands. Here, behind a dense thicket on the crest of a hill, was posted a strong force of as hardy troops as almost ever fought, almost perfectly protected by the conformation of the ground, and by logs and other rude and hastily prepared defences. To assail it an open field had to be passed, enfiladed by the fire of its batteries. It was nicknamed by the Confederates, by a very mild metaphor, 'The Hornets' Nest.' No fig-

114

ure of speech would be too strong to express the deadly peril of assault upon this natural fortress, whose inaccessible barriers blazed for six hours with sheets of flame and whose infernal gates poured forth a murderous storm of shot and shell and musket-fire, which no living thing could quell or even withstand. Brigade after brigade was led against it. But valor was of no avail. Hindman's brilliant brigades, which had swept everything before them from the field, were shivered into fragments in the shock of the assault, and paralyzed for the remainder of the day. A. P. Stewart's regiments made fruitless assaults, but only to retire mangled and disheartened.

"Bragg now ordered up [Randall Lee] Gibson's splendid brigade, composed of the 1st Arkansas, 4th, 13th, and 19th Louisiana, which moved forward with alacrity. Gibson himself, a knightly soldier, as gentle and courteous as he was unflinching, was aided by colonels, three of whom afterwards became generals. The brigade made a gallant charge, but, like the others, recoiled from the fire it encountered. A blaze of musketry swept through it from front to flank; powerful batteries were also opened upon its left. Under this cross-fire it at last fell back with very great loss. Allen's 4th Louisiana was dreadfully cut up in this charge, and suffered more confusion from a misapprehension that it was fired upon by friends. Gibson asked for artillery to be sent him; but it was not at hand,

and Bragg sent orders to charge again. The colonels thought it hopeless; but Gibson led them on to the attack, and they again suffered a bloody repulse.

"Gibson, who, assisted by [Henry W.] Allen and Avegno, had been leading the 4th and 13th Louisiana in the first two assaults, learning from the adjutant of [James F.] Fagan that the regiments on the right had suffered equal disaster, turned over the command of his left wing to Colonel Allen, with directions to execute the orders received from General Bragg. He then proceeded to the right and helped Fagan to lead the magnificent 1st Arkansas again to the assault.

"Four times the position was charged; four times the assault proved unavailing. The brigade was repulsed, but maintained its ground steadily, until Wallace's position was turned, when, again renewing its forward movement in conjunction with Cheatham's command, it helped to drive back its stout opponents. Lieut.-Colonel Thompson, of the 1st Arkansas, fell pierced with seven balls. Two of its captains were killed; the major, a captain, and many officers, wounded. In the 4th Louisiana, Colonel Allen was wounded, and three captains and three lieutenants killed or wounded. Gibson's entire staff was disabled, and his assistant adjutant-general, Colonel Ben King, killed. When Gibson went to Fagan, Allen, a very fearless soldier, wrung at his unavailing loss, rode back to General Bragg to repeat the need of artillery, and to ask him if he must charge again. Bragg, impatient at the check, hastily replied, 'Colonel Allen, I want no faltering now.' Allen, stung by the reply, said not a word, but, going back to his command, and waving his sword for his men to follow, charged once more, but again in vain. He never forgave Bragg, and the brigade thought they got hard measure in Bragg's orders and in his report.

"Patton Anderson's brigade, with the Crescent Regiment, of Pond's brigade, aided by a regiment, battalions, and a battery from Trabue's brigade, were eventually more successful farther to the left. His ground was also very difficult, but he caught the enemy more on the flank, and clung to it, rattling them with musketry and artillery, until the movement of the Confederate right broke into this citadel, when he carried his point. But this was not until after hours of manœuvering and a heavy skirmishing with great loss, and after the enemy's left was turned. The 20th Louisiana was badly cut up in the under-brush, and in other regiments many companies lost all their officers."

Colonel Johnston is correct in his description of this portion of the battle, excepting that there was no citadel, fortifications, or other protection, beside that afforded by the banks of the old road along which the battle raged and the invincible valor of the brave men who were fighting for the unity of the nation.

Hurlburt was forced back, Wallace was killed after giving orders to cut their way through, his command having been surrounded; but Prentiss stood his ground until ammunition had been exhausted and a murderous fire was mowing his ranks from all sides, when he surrendered.

The first day's battle at Shiloh consisted of a series of detached conflicts, hardly less desperate than the one here described. What would have been the result had Lew Wallace come upon the field with his five thousand veteran troops, it is useless to speculate. On the night of the 6th, Buell came, and on the next day Beauregard's army was driven back and the Union forces regained in position and trophies what had been lost before, but more than twenty thousand men of both armies had been placed *hors du combat*, and thus ended one of the most desperate conflicts of the entire war of the Rebellion.

# THE CAPTURE OF
## New Orleans

*T*here is a bend in the Mississippi River, seventy miles below New Orleans and thirty miles from the Gulf of Mexico, where the mighty river sweeps first to the right and then to the left. The banks are but a few feet above high-water mark, bare in spots and marshy; then again, heavily wooded to the water's edge with gloomy moss-draped cypress and sturdy oak. There the Spaniards erected on the left bank Fort St. Philip, to which extensive additions were made in 1812-15 by the government. With Fort Jackson on the right, these two forts defied all hostile passage to the city over which they stood guard; and so strong is the natural position here, that in 1815 a sin-

gle fort held in check the entire British force for nine days.

In April, 1862, when [Admiral David Glasgow] Farragut's fleet of 6 sloops of war, 16 gun-boats, 18 mortar schooners, and 3 storeships appeared in the river, these forts had an armament of 128 guns and about 1,500 men, with a fleet of 13 gunboats and two iron-clad rams mounting 17 guns. Just below Fort Jackson there swung across the channel a line of hulks, chained together and anchored against the swift current. For six days, before the passage of the forts was attempted, the mortar schooners, under the gallant Porter, had, under cover of the woods below the bend, rained their incessant torrent of mortar shells. These huge bombs, weighing 285 pounds, after describing an immense arc in mid-air, plunged down into the doomed Fort Jackson, rending the parapets, dismounting guns, and opened the river banks till the water flooded the interior.

On the night of the 20th, Fleet-Captain Bell, with the "Pinola" and "Itasca," succeeded in breaking a passage in the obstructions sufficient for the fleet to go through. At two o'clock on the morning of April 24, two red lights were displayed at the peak of the flag-ship "Hartford," which was the signal for the fleet to weigh anchor and prepare for forcing a passage past the forts, in accordance with orders previously issued by Farragut. It was half past three, however, before the fleet got under way, and the watchful enemy had started their floating fire-rafts, and illumined each side of the river with huge bonfires, which, with the light of the moon, now risen, rendered the advancing fleet perfectly visible.

Porter, with his gun-boats, moved forward, and forming in line below the water batteries of Fort Jackson, poured in such a steady and galling fire that they were almost silenced. Capt. Bailey, with the First Division, consisting of the "Cayuga," "Pensacola," "Mississippi," "Oneida," "Varuna," "Katahdin," "Kineo," and "Wissahickon," after passing the obstructions, headed directly for Fort St. Philip under a tremendous fire from both forts, which did not slacken until the broadsides from the ships drove the artillerists from their guns. Above the batteries the rebel gun-boats were encountered, when there ensued a most desperate conflict, in which the vessels became intermixed, ramming and battering each other, while both sides made efforts to carry by boarding. It was during this struggle that the "Oneida" and "Varuna" rescued the "Cayuga" from the combined rebel fleet. The "Oneida" ran at full speed into one of their vessels, cut her almost in two, reducing her to a helpless wreck. The "Varuna," which was rammed by the "Gov. Moore" and "Stonewall Jackson," was finally sunk near the shore. The "Pensacola's" heavy broadsides did great execution, although she lost thirty-seven men from the heavy fire received while passing the forts. The "Mississippi" had encountered the turtle-backed ram "Manassas," received a terrific blow from her, but which did not prove a fatal injury. The ram, however, was finally riddled with shot, and sent adrift down the river, where she blew up. The rest of the division worked their way up through the smoke-darkened river past the forts, in time to take a hand in the battle above.

The "Hartford," bearing Flag-Officer Farragut, led the Second Division, consisting of the flagship, the "Brooklyn," and

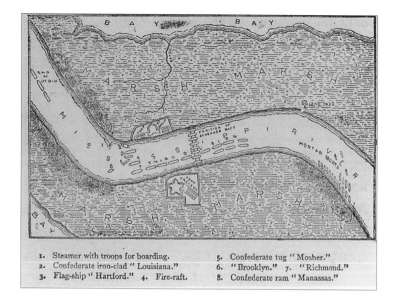

1. Steamer with troops for boarding.
2. Confederate iron-clad " Louisiana."
3. Flag-ship " Hartford." 4. Fire-raft.
5. Confederate tug " Mosher."
6. " Brooklyn." 7. " Richmond."
8. Confederate ram " Manassas."

"Richmond." She opened with her bow guns on Fort Jackson, when both forts responded with a terrific cross-fire, and the smoke and darkness of that terrible scene were illumined by the lurid blaze from the roaring throats of over two hundred cannon. A few minutes later, while avoiding a huge fire-raft at this place, the "Hartford" was sheered by the swift current and grounded close under the guns of Fort St. Philip.[1] The "Brooklyn," while extricating herself from an entanglement with the hulks, was terribly cut up by the forts and then battered by the

1. It is this point of that memorable and desperate battle which the picture represents. When the flag-ship went aground, the Confederate tug "Mosher" pushed a great fire-raft against her side, which set her on fire; the iron-clad "Louisiana," under her bows, raked her through and through; and Fort St. Philip increased her fire with frightful rapidity. The crew of the "Hartford" fought with desperation, and her heavy broadsides were hurled into the fort as rapidly as human hands could man the guns. Her deck was a glare of light; the flames were hissing and leaping along her sides, through the ports and up into the rigging. "Don't flinch from that fire, boys," coolly called out Farragut, to the firemen who were fighting the flames; "there's a hotter place than that for those who don't do their duty!" Fearing neither destruction nor capture, he turned his forecastle gun upon a steamer with troops preparing to board the ship, sending a shell crashing through the steamer's decks, completely wrecking her. The rebel ram "Manassas," coming down from the fight above, ran into the "Hartford"; the force of the blow, however, proved a providential assistance in clearing her from the bar, and she then fought her way out of this perilous position. Above and around the doomed forts arise light-encircling wreaths from bursting shells, broken by the serpent-like trails of descending bombs hurled through mid-air from Porter's mortars two miles away; while through this lurid glare is seen a glimpse of the clear blue starlit sky, in striking contrast to the scene below.

"Manassas," but her tremendous broadsides kept down partially the fire of the forts while she was passing them.

The Third Division under Capt. Bell, consisting of the "Sciota," "Iroquois," "Kennebec," "Pinola," "Itasca," and "Winona," now came up in their order, meeting the floating wrecks, fire-rafts, and débris of the fight above. The first three hastened by the forts during a pause in the battle, and escaped comparatively unharmed. It was daylight before these got well into the fight, and the "Itasca," "Winona," and "Kennebec" were cut off by the Confederate fire, which opened anew after the main fleet had passed. Of these, the "Itasca" was shot through the boiler, and so completely riddled that she had to be abandoned.

Farragut's main object, that of forcing a passage by the forts, had, however, been accomplished. The main portion of the squadron were now above them, and steaming up towards New Orleans.

When the sun rose the morning after the fight, the forts were still unsubdued, and the great ram "Louisiana" lay at her berth beside Fort St. Philip, almost unharmed, and with her, several river steamers remaining to dispute the passage of the rest of the Federal fleet which lay below. Commander Porter was now in imminent danger, for he was left with only the mortar fleet, the altered ferry-boats "Westfield " and "Clifton," the gun-boats "Owasco," "Harriet Lane," "Pinola," "Winona," and "Kennebec," to contend with the two forts and rebel fleet, but no hesitation marked his actions. Immediate preparations were made for a renewed attack with his little fleet. The mortar vessels opened fire and bombarded the fort during the 25th, while five were sent round in the Gulf to attack in the rear, and preparations were made to capture the "Louisiana" at close quarters with the gun-boats. The garrisons of the forts now became discouraged and mutinous, and refusing to fight any longer, the forts surrendered, not, however, before the famous "Louisiana" had been set on fire and drifted down to explode near the Union fleet. On the morning of the 25th, Farragut's ships ranged up abreast of New Orleans, the Empire City of the South, demanding her surrender to the Union fleet. And thus, in the flaming fires at Fort St. Philip and Fort Jackson, was forged the first link in the giant chain with which the government was to surround the entire Confederacy.

# BATTLE BETWEEN THE

## "*Monitor*" AND "*Merimac*"

MARCH 9, 1862

No war-ship in history has been surrounded by such romance and popular interest as the little ironclad Monitor that fought the Merrimac and saved the North, in 1862. Nelson's ship, the Victory, and many other historic ships, have been preserved carefully to the present day; but of the Monitor we have nothing but the memory of her wonderful birth, her first and great battle, and tragic loss.

Imagination loves to dwell on those days in '62, so crowded with events tremendous in meaning to our national existence. The Merrimac had dragged her great black length down from Norfolk, and on her trial trip to Newport News had demon-strated her resistless power by utterly destroying two of the government's finest frigates. The Cumberland and Congress received her with the bravery for which our sailors have ever been noted; but not until the former had received her death-wound and hoisted the blood-red flag of "no surrender," as her broadsides tore along the enemy's impenetrable sides search-ing for some vital spot, even as the water closed over the guns, did the Confederates pause aghast at the spirit of desperate resistance their attack had aroused.

How few, amid the gloom and silence that enshrouded the Union fleet and fortress that night, realized that the little black object working along the coast at midnight, whose crew had heard the guns and seen the fires of the burning Congress, was the Monitor, hastening to their deliverance from a second attack and total destruction! When the Merrimac crossed the bay early next morning to complete her work, this conqueror of two frigates found her way unexpectedly barred by a new foe.[1]

The Merrimac, although 310 feet long, showed above water but her iron-clad overpart, which was 170 feet long, 50 feet wide and 7 high, with ten guns. Her appearance when moving through the water was as that of some huge marine monster.

The Monitor was a raft, only one foot above water, with a central tower, whose inside diameter was 20 feet, height 9 feet, and thickness 8 inches of iron. The side armor was 5 inches, deck 1 inch; her guns threw shot of 180 pounds. Her speed was 7 knots.

It was apparent early in the struggle that the Monitor was the swifter and more easily managed, for she circled about her huge antagonist, heading her off, running close to her and away at will, planting her shot deliberately, and testing with mighty strokes all her antagonist's powers of defence as coolly

---

1. Mr. Francis B. Butts of Providence, R.I., a participant in that engagement, says in a recent letter: "At 5.30 A.M., all hands were called, and the ship was immediately cleared of her sea rig and got ready for battle. Shot were hoisted into the turret, and a thorough inspection made, that everything about the ship should be in working order. Breakfast over, all was quiet and solemn, as if preparing for a funeral. At 7.30 o'clock a long line of black smoke was seen issuing from the Merrimac, which was preceded by her consorts, the steamers Jamestown, Patrick Henry, and Teazer. It was the signal for battle. The crews of the different vessels stood by their guns, fusees in hand. The Monitor steamed slowly from beneath the bows of the Minnesota, where she had been partially concealed, to meet the challenger in an open contest. It was an astonishment to the rebels and our own people alike. Neither had seen her when she arrived, and many were the conjectures of what she could be. Some said a huge water-tank, others an infernal machine; none that she had guns, and not till they saw steam rise from her deck did they think she had power to move herself. Onward, with the brave [John L.] Worden at her wheel, she was steered straight for the Merrimac, whose consorts, loaded with spectators and soldiers cheering with victory, had dropped astern and out of the channel. Onward, in a straight line, the Monitor kept her course. Her diminutive size, for only the turret could be seen by those who were a mile or more away, seemed like a rat attacking an alligator. The Merrimac stopped her engines as if to survey and wonder at the audacity of the nondescript (the Monitor) which was approaching on her starboard bow. Then, as if seized with impulsive rage, and as if a puff of her huge cannon would sweep her away, the Merrimac poured a simultaneous broadside of solid shot at her. For an instant she was enveloped in a dense smoke, and those who were looking on held their breath in doubt of ever seeing the Monitor again. It was a moment of great suspense; then, as a gentle breeze swept over the scene, the Monitor appeared. At this instant the flash of her own guns was seen, and their report, louder than any cannon that had ever been heard, thundered across the sea. It seemed to jar the very earth, and the iron scales of the "invincible" rumbled and cracked from their fastenings. One on board of the Merrimac at the time has told me that, though at first entirely confident of victory, consternation took hold of them all. 'D——n it,' said one, 'the thing is full of guns.' The enthusiasm at this moment among the thousands of civilians and soldiers, who lined the shores to witness the fight, was beyond description and their own control. Such a spontaneous burst of cheers was never before heard. Men were frantic with joy, and fell into one another's embrace, or upon their knees in grateful thanks to the God of battles for his mercy and deliverance."

122

as a trained gladiator. It was no longer only the frantic struggle of a wooden frigate, striving to damage her foe as much as possible before sinking, but a combat with a determined duellist, that parried blows, gave cut for thrust, dodged and retreated as the fight required, keenly watching her chances and planting blows with unerring accuracy and power.

What wonderful sights must have been presented within those hulls as they wheeled about in that mortal struggle. The officers and men working at the guns, the gunners stripped to the waist, the engineers at their posts of duty, the pilots watching the channel's shoals and tides, while deep down in the bowels of each, scores of coal-begrimed firemen fed the huge furnaces amid hiss of steam and glare of fires. Orders from officers, and answering shouts of the men, could scarcely be heard amid the explosions of the great guns overhead, and the terrible detonations of shot against the turret. Still, through stifling heat and choking smoke, these men fought on.

To the spectators crowded about that immense bay the sight was grand and exciting. The hot sun's rays poured down on the unruffled waters of the arena, where in the centre arose and drifted slowly off billowy clouds of smoke from which shot brilliant tongues of flame and mighty thunders of cannon. Now the Merrimac would appear for a moment through the drifting smoke, closely followed in some evolution by the little Monitor; again both would disappear in the pall of vapor, above and through which constantly showed the waving trail of smoke from the Merrimac's funnel, like a black cloud against the sky. When either combatant afforded a target, the surrounding forts and ships on the outskirts of the fight let drive their batteries, to damage perchance by some lucky shot the opposing champion, and both vessels were repeatedly struck by these missiles, which tore the water about them.

For six hours this terrific fight progressed before either showed signs of exhaustion. At this time the Monitor's turret was dented by shot, her decks scored and strewn with flattened and broken balls, and pilot-house burst open to the light of day. The Merrimac looked a wreck. Her outer covering had been partially swept off; boats, flag-staff, funnel, rails, everything smashed by shot; and her sides were shattered and opened by the tremendous pounding. One eleven-inch shot, fired by the Monitor but thirty feet distant, struck half-way up the shield, and nearly burst in her side of twenty-eight inches of oak and iron. Forty of her crew were swept off their feet by the concussion. The Merrimac paused. For six hours she had striven to fight down or sweep out of the way that little Monitor, yet there she remained defiant as ever, refusing to stop or fly. It was too much for the conqueror of the day before, and she retired.

Some authorities claim that if the Merrimac had not left her ram in the side of the Cumberland, and had two guns disabled in the previous engagement, she would have towed the Monitor into Norfolk a prize; but when we remember that the Monitor's gunners used but fifteen-pound charges of powder instead of thirty, as were afterwards used in the same guns, we can judge of how narrow an escape the Merrimac had from being shattered to pieces and sunk by the little Monitor, this production of Ericsson's genius, which rendered useless the existing war-ships of Europe and America and revolutionized the building of navies forever.

ARTIST'S NOTE.—In regard to the composition of the picture, Mr. Davidson, the artist, says: "In painting the Monitor and Merrimac, I obtained valuable and authentic information from Commander, then lieutenant, S. Dana Greene, who fought the Monitor's guns; also from personal criticisms of the work by Capt. John Ericsson, of New York City, inventor of the Monitor. Descriptions and drawings of the Merrimac were furnished by her constructor, Mr. John L. Porter, of Norfolk Va., and other information obtained from articles written by John Taylor Wood, lieutenant of the Merrimac. Additional information and facts regarding the engagement were secured from descriptions and sketches by Mr. F. A. Silva, marine painter, who was then in the United States army, and a witness of the battle from Newport News. The view given in the illustration is near the close of the fight, when the Monitor, ranging alongside the Merrimac, is firing at short range, to crush through the iron casement."

# BATTLE OF
## *Mobile Bay*

Ere daylight streaked the horizon on that memorable Aug. 5, 1864, the boatswain's pipes rose shrilly, calling "all hands up hammocks" through Farragut's squadron, which since January had blockaded Mobile Bay. For months both land and naval forces had been gathering for a final effort to burst the doors of this great Southern entry port for war supplies, and outlet of cotton. The night before, the monitor "Tecumseh," the last to arrive, steamed in from sea, and all was ready. At daylight the fleet was moving swiftly in; the wooden vessels, fourteen in number, lashed together in couples; with the four monitors abreast of the head of the line on the right, the six gunboats remaining outside to shell the fort in flank. What did the Admiral expect to do with that fleet going in on the flood tide with the morning mists about them? He had determined to force a passage through the narrow channel close to the fort and water batteries, with their one hundred and seventeen cannons and six hundred and forty men, against the Confederate fleet, consisting of their famous ironclad ram "Tennessee," the gunboats "Selma," "Gaines," and "Morgan," and withal to avoid the one hundred submerged torpedoes, to strike and explode any one of which meant instant destruction to the vessel above it.

As the "Tecumseh" ranged the fort, she opened fire, and it replied with a storm of shot, and for a full half-hour the entire fleet was subjected to a dead-ahead raking fire that tore through the masts and rigging like a storm through a forest. What a sublime scene the decks of those ships must have presented as they glided in where the channel leads them, head on, into that flaming circle of shot and shell, the crews bravely standing like grim statues beside their glistening guns, ready for the signal to fire! On the "Hartford" a shot shatters the mast above them as with a lightning-stroke; a rifle shell pierces her side between two forward nine-inch guns, killing and wounding fifteen men; another cuts a swath fore and aft through her crowded decks. The dead lie as they fall; the wounded crawl gasping out of the way; the living stand with blanched faces and clinched teeth watching through the smoke the grand old Admiral in the shrouds and the quartermasters at the wheel, whose next movement may bring them broadside to the fort.

The "Oneida's" boilers are pierced and her crew terribly scalded, but she struggles on into the fight, assisted by the "Galena." All the ships are now receiving a terrific fire. Suddenly, as the "Tecumseh" reaches abreast of the fort, a hidden torpedo explodes directly beneath her. She lurches once, twice, then drops out of sight beneath the waves. A column of smoke and spray rushes up as she disappears, and of the one

hundred and thirty men composing her crew, but seventeen rise to the surface. Appalled at the sight, the "Brooklyn" stops and backs, the closely following vessels forge ahead, crowding each other, and a terrible confusion seems inevitable. While in this position they are helpless under the guns of the fort; and while their own broadsides are silent, the smoke clears away somewhat, revealing their dilemma. The foe, with renewed energy, opens his batteries, "and the whole of Mobile Point," says an eye-witness, "bursts into a living flame." "What's the trouble?" calls Farragut to the "Brooklyn," now close aboard and backing. "Torpedoes ahead!" comes the answer. "Damn the torpedoes! Four bells! Go ahead full speed! Give her all the steam you've got!" Someone must risk the submerged danger, and the Admiral rushes his own vessel into the lead. The line straightens out abreast of the fort, the command to fire runs along the decks, and the long silent broadsides burst from the ships in sheets of flame. The guns of the water batteries are overthrown, the casements and parapets of the fort tossed about in great fragments, and the artillerists mowed down by the iron tempest. Now the "Brooklyn" wheels and delivers her fire, then the "Richmond," and the "Lackawanna," "Monongahela," "Ossipee," and "Oneida" follow in close succession, swelling the storm, and each carrying her consort alongside on

125

the swift inflowing tide. The decks are covered with dead and wounded, and débris of splintered wood and iron. Some are on fire, but the crews ram home their charges, and hurl their shot into the fort with cheers, for the crisis is over, and they have drawn by the terrible torpedoes.

126

As the squadron heads up the bay, the Confederate gunboats turn to flee. The "Morgan," under cover of a rain-squall, wheels and runs back to the fort. The "Selma," chased by the "Itasca," "Metacomet," "Port Royal," and "Kennebec," surrenders. The "Gaines" runs aground, and is burned near the fort.

Scarcely has the fleet anchored when the ironclad "Tennessee" comes single-handed to combat them all. Slipping their cables, Farragut's ships are instantly under way to meet her, separating fan wise on either side to gain headway and position for ramming. First to rush upon and strike her is the "Monongahela," whose iron bow is destroyed by the shock; then the "Lackawanna" nearly sinks herself in a like attempt; then the "Hartford" strikes a tremendous blow. The ram, thus met with her own tactics, turns to escape, but is edged across the bay by the crowding wooden ships and slower monitors, where, in a pocket of the shoaling water, she is rammed by the ships and pounded with shot until helpless; and with the monitor "Chickasaw" across her stern, the "Winnebago" ahead,

and the rest of the fleet coming head on to run her down, she at last surrenders.

On the 6th, Fort Powell was evacuated and blown up, Fort Morgan surrendered on the 23d after a bombardment by the fleet, and Farragut was master of Mobile Bay.

This great victory cost the Union fleet three hundred and thirty-five men, and one hundred and seventy men wounded, many being injured on the wooden vessels by the splinters which filled the air, coming in cords, and in size sometimes were like logs of wood.

The destruction of the "Tecumseh" was due to the eagerness of her commander to meet the "Tennessee," which was then bearing down upon them. He ordered his pilot to slightly change his course, and by so doing, struck the fatal buoy, and she went down with nearly every soul on board. The pilot, John Collins, and Commander Craven met at the foot of the ladder leading to the top of the turret. Knowing that it was by his own command that the fatal change had been made, Craven stepped aside and said, "After you, pilot." "But," said the pilot in repeating the incident, "there was nothing after me, for when I reached the top of the ladder the vessel seemed to drop from under me."

The romantic incident of Farragut being lashed to the mast

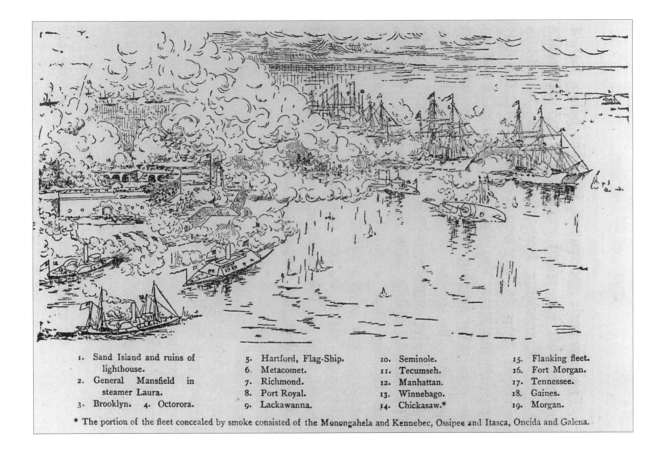

| | | | |
|---|---|---|---|
| 1. Sand Island and ruins of lighthouse. | 5. Hartford, Flag-Ship. | 10. Seminole. | 15. Flanking fleet. |
| | 6. Metacomet. | 11. Tecumseh. | 16. Fort Morgan. |
| 2. General Mansfield in steamer Laura. | 7. Richmond. | 12. Manhattan. | 17. Tennessee. |
| | 8. Port Royal. | 13. Winnebago. | 18. Gaines. |
| 3. Brooklyn.  4. Octorora. | 9. Lackawanna. | 14. Chickasaw.* | 19. Morgan. |

\* The portion of the fleet concealed by smoke consisted of the Monongahela and Kennebec, Ossipee and Itasca, Oneida and Galena.

has raised controversy and difference of opinion, resulting from the fact that he seldom remained long in any one position. As the fleet was drawing near the fort, the Admiral stood in the port main rigging, where he could see all about him. As the smoke increased, he, step by step, ascended the rigging above the futtock bands. The captain seeing him in this perilous position, and fearing that a shock might precipitate him into the sea, sent a sailor to pass a line around him and make it fast to a forward and after shroud, and in this position the Admiral remained until the fleet had passed the fort.

# *Kearsarge* AND *Alabama*

## HAULING DOWN THE FLAG

The Civil War in the United States, 1861-65, was largely waged upon the land. The operations on the water were marked by the vigilance and discretion required in blockading service, the ability and gallantry necessary to the reduction of coast defences, and the display of individual terrorism like that of the lamented "Albemarle" Cushing.

There were no great sea-fights like Trafalgar, but the professional qualities which Nelson and Farragut possessed were often brought into play, as in front of New Orleans, in Hampton Roads, and on the high seas, near Cherbourg, France.

It is a peculiarity of the naval history of that war that it comprises two of the most famous naval duels of any time; the one, "Monitor" and "Merrimac," marking the first chapter, and the other, "Kearsarge" and "Alabama," near the end of the bloody volume.

Mr. Davidson has chosen the final scene in the last-named affair as the subject of his picture,—the moment when the "Alabama," "the scourge of American commerce," yields to superior marksmanship, and strikes her colors.

To fully appreciate the importance of this act it is proper to note here, briefly, the career of the Confederate cruiser.

The "Alabama" was built in 1862 by John Laird, a famous English ship-builder, and was originally called "The 290." It is said that she represented, when completed, the strongest and swiftest type of war vessel of her day and size afloat, being a model of symmetry and buoyancy. She was rated at nine hundred tons' burden, and measured two hundred and thirty feet in length, thirty two feet beam, and when supplied for a cruise, drew fifteen feet of water. Her spars included long lower masts, enabling her to carry large fore and aft sails, so important to a steamer. In speed she was estimated at ten knots, although she made eleven and a half knots on her trial trip. Her armament consisted of six thirty-two pounders in broadside and two pivot guns—one a hundred-pounder Blakely rifle, and the other a long eight-inch smooth bore; a total of eight guns.

The crew of this famous freebooter numbered one hundred and twenty men and twenty-four officers; the men were largely of the fillibuster type, of divers [sic] nationalities, while the officers were generally Americans.

The commander of this gallant rover was Capt. Raphael Semmes, formerly an officer of the United States Navy.

The "Alabama" hoisted "the stars and bars" at sea, about Sept. 1, 1862, and entered upon her career of spoliation. She commenced with the Yankee whaler "Ocmulgee," of Edgartown, and ended on the 27th of April, 1864, with the capture and burning of the "Tycoon," of New York. During that period more than forty-five American merchantmen were overhauled and scuttled or burned to the water's edge by this cruiser, without any interruption from the navy of the United States.

The extent of the service rendered to his government by Capt. Semmes is indicated by the indemnity paid after the war by Great Britain to Uncle Sam, for allowing the "Alabama" and other cruisers to be constructed at a British dock-yard, and failing to prevent their departure upon a hostile errand. This lack of vigilance cost John Bull the neat little sum of $15,500,000.

The story of the "Alabama's" two-years' raid teems with incidents akin in many respects to those of successful piracy; if there was no murder, there was the destroying torch; if stern discipline was enforced above deck, below at times, we are told, reigned the genius of misrule, and the motley crew sought a vent for their hot blood and rough spirit by brutal broils and moblike contention.

The romance which often tinges the profession of "gentlemen of the road" came more than once to the surface, as when the California steamer, with nails and passengers, was overhauled on the briny turnpike in November, 1862.

130

This vessel had been completely deceived by the sight of the friendly stars and stripes which rippled from the peak of the "Alabama." As that ship appeared in her true colors, the passengers, among whom were many women and children, became greatly alarmed. But Capt. Semmes, having in his youth read Cooper's sea novels, in an iron-hand-in-velvet-glove spirit detailed a light-waisted middy, with a gold-laced uniform and a silver tongue, to allay the fears of the trembling ladies. This commission was executed with such success that tears were soon dried, toilets were touched up, Cupid prepared to capture Mars (or Neptune), and it is currently reported that when the young ambassador was finally recalled he was found ensconced in a corner with the prettiest of the fair captives expounding appropriate lines from the "Corsair" in the strict performance of his duty.

> *"He sees his bark, he notes how fair the wind,*
> *And sternly gathers all his might of mind;*
> *Again he hurries on, and as he hears*
> *The clang of tumult vibrate on his ears,*
> *The busy sounds, the bustle of the shore,*
> *The shout, the signal, and the dashing oar;*
> *As marks his eye the sea-boy on the mast,*
> *The anchors rise, the sails unfurling fast,*

> *The waving kerchiefs of the crowd that urge*
> *That mute adieu to those who stem the surge,*
> *And more than all, his blood-red flag aloft,*
> *He marvell'd how his heart could seem so soft."*

Upon another occasion (the only one, it is said, before the final exit of the "Alabama") when that vessel trusted herself within short range of a United States man-of-war, the customs of civilized warfare were ignored by Captain Semmes, and he was enabled to sink the U.S. steamer "Hatteras," an iron side-wheel river boat, transformed into a gunboat, while displaying false colors, and holding a parley of the nature of a flag of truce. However, a day of reckoning for the "Alabama" was approaching.

On the eleventh day of June, 1864, that vessel anchored in the harbor of Cherbourg, and on the 14th the United States steamer "Kearsarge," Capt. John A. Winslow, arrived, and after communicating with the local authorities, placed herself on guard just off the entrance to the port.

This action of Capt. Winslow was equivalent to a challenge to fight or surrender, and as the brave Confederate could not afford, under the circumstances, to avoid a conflict, he followed suit by asking the Union commander to do what that officer was already doing, to await the "Alabama's" movements.

131

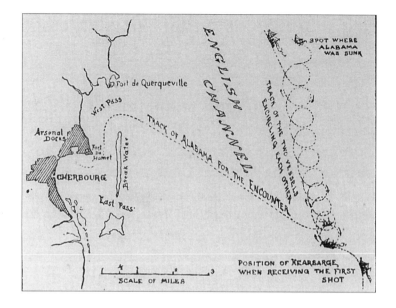

132

During the next three or four days the busy note of preparation was heard on both vessels, in protecting the engines and in stripping the ships of superfluous top-hamper. On the "Alabama" the machinery was fortified by the coal bunkers, while the commander of the "Kearsarge" had improvised a coat of chain mail for his ship, by hanging sheet chains along her sides. The ships were almost equal in armament and numbers of crew. The "Kearsarge" carried seven guns, throwing projectiles of the aggregate weight of four hundred and thirty pounds, while the "Alabama" had eight guns, or three hundred and sixty pounds of shot and shell. The "Yankee" crew was one hundred and sixty-three strong, against one hundred and forty-nine "Rebels."

Sunday, the 19th, arrived, and the "Kearsarge," still cruising off the entrance to the harbor, awaited any movement of her foe. It was a fine day, the atmosphere slightly hazy. The crew, dressed in their Sunday suits, had been inspected at quarters and dismissed for divine service. Capt. Winslow was conducting the service below when the officer of the deck shouted down the hatch, "The Alabama; she's coming!" Dropping the prayer-book, he grasped his trumpet, ordered the ship cleared for action and headed seaward. It was to be a duel *à outrance*, as it seemed to the volatile natives, who lined the heights overlooking the town; to the commander of the English yacht "Deerhound," acting as a sort of second to the "Alabama"; and to the gallant Gaul who, from the bridge of the French iron-clad "Couronne," surveyed the field as umpire and international policeman.

Semmes harangued his officers and crew in Napoleonic fashion, assuring them that "the name of your ship has become a household word wherever civilization extends. Shall that name be tarnished by defeat? The thing is impossible."

The "Kearsarge" drew off shore a few miles, followed by her antagonist; then turning, she was saluted by a shot from the "Alabama," which fell short. The "Kearsarge" steamed full head for her enemy, and at nine hundred yards delivered a broadside from her starboard battery. Then followed manœuvres for position, the opponents describing a series of circles presenting their starboard batteries to each other, and keeping up a continuous fire for more than an hour. Both vessels were beautifully handled, so far as navigation went; but the superiority of the fire from the "Kearsarge" was apparent early in the fight.

Her guns were handled with skill and precision, and aimed to strike near the water line. The effect of the fire was plainly visible from the "Kearsarge," and with every telling shot the crew wildly cheered. Finally, a dexterous move of that vessel brought her enemy "in chancery."

Mr. Davidson depicts the scene at this moment when (as he says) *"The 'Alabama' had attempted with sails set to escape to port. The 'Kearsarge' is throwing herself across her bows for a raking position, and then was seen the Confederate flag being lowered in token of their surrender.* I show the after 11-inch pivot gun of the 'Kearsarge,' which did so much damage to the enemy. The gun's crew have just run it out loaded, ready for firing; when the enemy's flag is seen descending, and the order has been given, 'cease firing.' The gunner has jumped upon the gun carriage to assure himself of the fact, and is shaking hands with a comrade. In his right hand is the lock-string, and on his thumb the half glove-finger (thumbstall) for closing the vent; his left hand, wounded and grimy with powder stains, is extended towards the enemy. Still hauling on the gun-tackle is a negro (there were several in the 'Kearsarge's' crew). On the deck, in a box, is one of the 11-inch shells, and a stand of canister intended for use at short range, while two men are bringing a solid shot from the magazine. The loader at the muzzle of the gun has thrown his rammer into the open port and waves his cap. A shell (authentic) has pierced the bulwarks, exploded, and wounded three of the crew. Two were able to go

133

below unaided; the other is being assisted by two comrades. Splinters from the bulwarks are scattered on the deck. The man at the tackle-and-fall has taken a turn on the cleat, and is lowering away a shell after hearing the order to 'cease firing.' A powder passer (in red shirt) with a cartridge in his arms has stopped on hearing it and awaits further orders. The gun crew forward have just fired their piece, and the loader is passing the sponger in preparing to load. In the noise and smoke they have not heard nor seen the surrender.

"On the left is seen the brave commander of the 'Kearsarge,' Capt. John A. Winslow. The officer, with sword in hand, is Lieut.-Commander James S. Thornton, the executive officer of the ship."

The casualties were principally confined to the "Alabama." An eleven-inch shell entered her side near the water line, tearing a hole through which the sea poured in a deluge. The boats of both vessels were nearly all rendered unserviceable by fragments of shell. Partly by reason of the "chain-mail," and partly by the poor gun practice of the enemy, the "Kearsarge" escaped with slight damage.

Thirty men of the "Alabama" were killed or wounded, and ten were drowned. On the "Kearsarge" but three men were wounded.

The "Deerhound" aided the boats of the victor in rescuing the vanquished from a watery grave, but with questionable propriety deprived Capt. Winslow of several prisoners, including the commander of the "Alabama."

The "Alabama" sunk in forty-five fathoms of water, about six miles off Cherbourg. Settling by the stern, the falling aft of her batteries and stores threw her bows high in the air, and down, stern foremost, to her final resting-place, disappeared "the terror of American commerce."

# PASSING THE BATTERIES AT

## *Port Hudson*

---

Admiral Farragut had passed the forts below New Orleans and opened the lower Mississippi, when his services were required in reorganizing the Union fleet at Pensacola. His absence from the field of active operations was soon cut short, however, by the news that the Confederates were heavily fortifying the bluffs at the bend in the Mississippi, at Port Hudson, and he hastened back to break the grasp which the enemy had here obtained on the river.

The batteries at this point had been reconnoitred by Lieut.-Commander R. B. Lowry, with the gun boats "Kineo" and "Sciota," as early as Nov. 15, 1862, and he mentions in his report of "having seen enough to decide that the place was strongly fortified, and was by nature the most formidable obstacle on the river. The plans of the fortifications appear to be to place their works in such a position that we, having passed or silenced one or more of the lower batteries, other concealed batteries open, which will throw a cross-fire into the stern of the vessels, which would then be exposed to a cross-fire from batteries as yet to be approached and silenced, and from the masked ones yet astern." At this point the river curves like a huge letter "S," with high bluffs on the right, surmounted for a plunging fire with cannon of the heaviest calibre, at an altitude, in most cases, too great to be reached by the fire from the ships; while to the left a low point and shoal banks render the danger of running aground imminent at all times, should the swift current turn the ships from their course.

Hastily collecting what vessels he could, Farragut arranged to attack the place in conjunction with General [Nathaniel P.] Banks, whose forces were investing it by land. On the evening of March 14, 1863, he was awaiting, in readiness with a fleet of four ships and three gun-boats, for the signal from Banks that he was ready to advance; while below lay the five mortar-boats with the ironclad "Essex " and steamer "Sachem."

The Admiral's general order to the fleet was as follows:—

"The ships will each take a gun-boat on her port side, and secure her as well aft as possible, so as to leave the port battery clear for the enemy's battery on the port side of the river, going up, after we round the point opposite Port Hudson.

"Each ship will keep a little on the starboard quarter of her next ahead, so as to give free range to her chase guns, without risk of damage from premature explosion of shrapnel or shell.

"The captains will bear in mind that the object is to run the batteries at the least possible damage to our ships, and thereby secure an efficient force above, for the purpose of rendering such assistance as may be required of us to the army at Vicksburg, or, if not required there, to our army at Baton Rouge. If they succeed in getting past the batteries, the gun-boats will proceed up to the mouth of Red River, and keep up police of the

river batteries between that river and Port Hudson, capturing everything they can. Should any vessel be disabled, so that she is unable to pass Port Hudson, she will use the gun-boat to the best advantage. If the captain thinks he can get by, try it; if he thinks not, let the gun-boat drop her down below the range of the batteries. If both are disabled, then club down with a light anchor, or use the sails, as in his judgment may seem best. But I expect all to go by who are able; and I think the best protection against the enemy's fire is a well-directed fire from our own guns, shell and shrapnel at a distance, and grape when within four hundred or five hundred yards.

"D. G. FARRAGUT, *Rear-Admiral.*"

The "Mississippi," being a side-wheeler, could not take a gun-boat alongside, but one was assigned to each one of the other ships, to be lashed to its side, the fastest gun-boat being given to the slowest ship, in the following order:—

HARTFORD (flag-ship)
ALBATROSS (gun-boat) } Capt. JAMES S. PALMER.
RICHMOND, Commander JAMES ALDEN.
GENESEE (gun-boat), Commander W. H. MACOMB.
MONONGAHELA, Capt. J. P. MCKINISKRY.
KINEO (gun-boat), Lieut.-Commander JOHN WATTERS.
MISSISSIPPI, Capt. MELANCTON SMITH.

By this arrangement the gun-boat could tow the larger ship should she be disabled, while the larger would protect it by its bulwarks from shot. All the ships were trimmed by the head, so they could the more easily back off if run aground, and the mortar schooners were directed to keep up a constant fire during the continuance of the action.

At five o'clock that afternoon the Admiral received a despatch from General Banks that he was ready to make the land attack, and as darkness closed over the turbid river, the signal to get under way was given amid the most solemn silence. What a sight was presented on the crowded decks of those grim war ships, as they silently answered the signal lights and moved up against the current to the attack! The gun-crews, half stripped, standing by their pieces; the gun-captains, lanyard in hand, waiting for the word to begin their deadly work; the men in the forecastles straining their eyes through the gloom to catch the first glimpse of the enemy; the engineers below carefully tending the smoothly turning engines; while still farther down in the ships are the firemen feeding their furnaces amid the stifling heat; and between decks the surgeons, with their glittering knives and instruments of mercy, await those whom the storm of war will soon lay helpless before them.

On they glide into the murky night and approach the batteries; are almost abreast of them, when a rocket from the right bank hisses up into the darkness, giving warning of their approach. It scarcely rises its full height when a volley from the west battery ploughs the water in furrows about the leading vessels. Another and another follow, until the entire river bank above them is in a sheet of flame. Then the fleet opens fire with the forward guns, followed by quick broadsides, and the air is filled with the howl of shells, the rush of solid shot, and crash of splintered wood. As the fleet enters the bend opposite the main forts, the belching smoke of the land batteries rolls down over the river and mingles with that of the naval guns, thus forming a vast canopy of blue-gray smoke, shutting out all view, hiding friend and foe alike from those on the river. On the land, however, it is different, for the gunners in the higher batteries can occasionally catch glimpses of the ships as they move like huge shadows through a fog, and, working their guns with desperate energy, pour their plunging fire into the arena before them with a certainty of hitting some one of the crowding vessels.

Through all this pandemonium of sound, there comes from below the regular beat and roar of the mortar-boats like a heavy bass accompaniment to the treble of the rifled guns. Dropping from out the murky heavens, followed by fiery trails of burning fuse, fall the great 13-inch shells, bursting just over the lower batteries, killing gunners with their fragments of iron, upsetting guns and tearing huge gaps in the parapets.

The artillerists desert these forts, and fleeing to those higher up the river renew their fire with increased energy. The fleet has at last reached a point abreast the town and is under the concentrated fire of the forts. The "Hartford," blinded by the smoke, loses her way and touches the bank right under the batteries. In a moment she stops her fire, and so soon as the rising smoke enables her to see her position backs off, and with a full head of steam glides on up stream, rounds the bend and is safe with her consort. Beacon fires now blaze up fitfully through the gloom along both shores, while locomotive head-lights, placed at intervals in front of the town, throw their glare through the battle smoke and enable the gunners to dis-cover the positions of the ships.

The "Hartford" and "Albatross" are safe, but where is the rest of the fleet? The "Richmond" had gained the bend and was almost in safety, when a solid shot struck her steam pipes near the safety valve, letting the steam escape. The "Genesee," her consort, was unable to carry both against the current; so, reluctantly, she turned back, and again taking the fire of the batteries, ran down to her anchorage below. Just before retir-ing, however, a torpedo skilfully placed in her track exploded under her stern, throwing up a heavy column of water, but doing no injury.

The "Monongahela," with the "Kineo" alongside was blinded in the smoke, and ran aground on the low point on the left bank, whereupon the "Kineo" broke her fastenings, run-ning ahead and aground also, carrying away in her course the "Monongahela's" port fore-brace, port foretop-mast, and top-gallant mast back-stay, the hammock nettings forward, and tearing the port sheet-anchor from its place. She then suc-ceeded in backing off, and giving her hawser to the "Monon-gahela," pulled her off the shoal, and both vessels started up stream again to follow the gallant "Hartford"; but scarcely had she proceeded half the distance ere her machinery became heated and she was forced to give up the fight and drop down to her anchorage by the mortar fleet.

The grand old frigate "Mississippi" was the most unfortunate of all that gallant fleet, for nothing remained of her but the memory of her glorious career when daylight broke over the river the next morning. Early she grounded on the same dan-gerous shoal which had proved so nearly fatal to the others, and being unable to back off, was burned and blown up. Sixty-four of her crew were missing, of whom twenty-four were probably killed. Captain Smith says in his report: "The 'Monongahela,' which was the next ahead, could not be seen. Supposing that she had increased her distance, the order was given to 'go ahead fast,' that we might close up. We had now reached the last and most formidable batteries and were congratulating ourselves upon having gained the turn, when the 'Mississippi' grounded and heeled over three streaks to port. The engine was immediately reversed, and the port guns (which had not been fired) were run in, to bring her on an even keel. The engine was backed for thirty-five minutes, and steam increased from thirteen to twenty-five pounds, which was considered by the engineer the greatest pressure the boilers would bear, when the pilot stated that it would be impossible to get the vessel off. I then ordered the port battery to be spiked, and with the pivot gun to be thrown overboard; but the latter was not accomplished until I deemed it most judicious to abandon the vessel, as the enemy had obtained our range, and we were exposed to the galling and crossfire of three batteries, their shot hulling us frequently. The sick and wounded were now ordered up, at which time we ceased firing, and three small boats (all we had) were immediately employed in landing the crew, while preparations were being made to destroy the vessel. Up to this time the men had been working the guns in the most splendid style, and aiming at every flash, which was the only guide to the location of the rebel works.... The crew were directed to throw overboard all the small arms, the engineer ordered to destroy the engine,

and the ship set fire in the forward store-room. To be positive that this was effectually done, the yeoman was sent below to make an examination, when three shots entered the storeroom, letting in the water and extinguishing the flames. She was then fired in four different places aft between decks. . . . I left the ship, accompanied by the first lieutenant, all having now been landed, and passed down to the 'Richmond' under the fire of the rebel batteries. At three o'clock A.M. the 'Mississippi' was observed to be afloat, and slowly drifting down the river, and at half past five she blew up, producing an awful concussion, which was felt for miles around."…

Thus ended this memorable battle; and although General Banks's attack on shore was repulsed and only two of Farragut's ships succeeded in getting above the forts, it must be regarded as a victory, for these vessels effectually opened and guarded the river above, and closed the mouth of the Red River from which the rebels derived their supplies.

Our picture represents that moment in the fight when the "Hartford" has reached safety above the forts, the "Monongahela" is turning to drift down, and the "Mississippi" is bursting into flame, as the crew desert her under the fire of the Confederate batteries.

# CAPTURE OF
## *Fort Fisher*

Fort Fisher, which guarded the entrance through Cape Fear River to the blockade runners' Mecca, Wilmington, N.C., was the most formidable fortification constructed by the Southern Confederacy. For nearly four years they had labored upon this defensive point, and by both friend and foe it had been pronounced impregnable. Those who had seen both places considered it stronger than the famous Malakoff at Sebastopol.

On the night of Dec. 23, 1864, was tried General [Benjamin F.] Butler's plan for blowing up the fort by exploding a vessel near shore containing two hundred tons of powder, but which resulted in a complete failure. At anchor, awaiting the result of this explosion, lay the squadron commanded by Admiral Porter. Early on the morning of the 24th was a busy time in the fleet, the crews having had their breakfast before daylight. The wind was light and off shore, the sea smooth, and the vessels took their assigned positions, opened fire, and when all got to work the bombardment was tremendous. Probably so severe a fire was never before concentrated upon a fort.

The fort consisted of a series of huge earthworks (similar to that shown in the foreground of the picture), extending about four hundred yards across the space from sea to river, and three times that distance along the sea front, in which at intervals were planted powerful batteries. During the day a pretty active fire was returned by the fort, most of which was directed at the wooden vessels. At night the fleet withdrew from range, and on the following day, Christmas, bright and early, were again in line and pounding away, the garrison answering from their Armstrongs, Blakeleys, and Columbiads with much greater vigor than on the day previous. The weather had changed on the 26th, and but little was done by either army or navy. General Butler, who was in charge of the land forces which were to co-operate with the navy, decided that an assault on the fort was not feasible, and further attempt by the navy at that time to reduce the fort had to be abandoned. On the 27th, the troops re-embarked in transports for Hampton Roads, but the same troops again returned on Jan. 12, under the command of General Terry. During the time a series of heavy gales had swept the coast, and a portion of the fleet had to find other anchorage. At intervals between the gales they had managed to replenish with coal and powder, and on the morning of Jan. 13, the bombardment of the fort again commenced, and the soldiers were landed some distance above. From the heavy and rapid fire returned from the fort, it was evident that the garrison had been re-enforced by both men and guns.

An excellent writer, who took part in the naval engagement, thus graphically describes the closing contest:—

"The 14th of January broke clear, with a smooth beach and light westerly wind. The iron-clads went in closer than ever, so that their keels were close to the sand,—impossible, except with perfectly smooth water,—and the bombardment commenced in a very business-like way. Some re-enforcements were observed to be thrown into the fort by a river steamer which had come down the Cape Fear River from Wilmington, and to-day the combatants were girding their loins for the final struggle, which every one felt to be near. By eleven in the morning the troops were all landed and intrenched among some scrubby woods about a mile and a half to the northward of the fort. South of this, toward the huge earthwork, there was an open space of sand and sedge for near a mile. At this time a storming party of sailors and marines pulled on shore from the fleet, and were soon landed, and about 2.30 the naval column was ready to advance along the beach, and at a given signal the fire of the fleet suddenly ceased, the quiet after such continuous uproar seeming quite unnatural.

"The naval column moved close along the beach by the left flank, with the intention of assaulting the face of the angle or main work, which was about forty feet high, and about like a railway embankment. In addition to these difficulties, there was a very strong stockade, bolted and battened and strapped together. Well, it was not a very pleasant job, but the sailors and marines marched down to try it.

141

142

"As the fire from the fleet ceased, the garrison came out of their bomb-proofs and manned the parapet of the sea-face of the fort, shooting at the sailors and marines from their 'coigne of vantage' as if the seafaring people were a covey of partridges. To a looker-on, the people who manned the parapet appeared only to fire the loaded pieces which were handed them by people in the rear; and the fire was not only rapid but accurate. The beach was soon full of dead and wounded, for there was no protection from the fire. Some of those wounded when very close to the water, staggered into the slight surf, and had to be assisted out. So heavy and fatal was this small-arm fire that few of the assaulting force actually reached the foot of the mound which formed the northeast angle of the fort. They could go no farther, and having reached a place of partial shelter at the foot of the sea-face of the fort, inside the stockade, they were obliged to stay there until the approaching darkness, and the hard fighting on the northern face of the fort drew the garrison off to the last man, and enabled the navy people to get away. In this foolhardy attempt twenty-one officers of the navy were killed and wounded, and the loss among the men was proportionate. As far as the assault went, it was a perfect failure; but the lives lost were not entirely thrown away, as the naval attack created a diversion, drawing the garrison off to the sea-face, dis-

tracting their attention, and allowing the preparations for the real assault to go on unmolested.

"About the time that it was evident that the naval attack was not to succeed, there emerged from the scrubby wood north of the fort the troops destined to assault the place. These were veterans from the Army of the James. Rough looking, with frowzy clothing and dishevelled hair and beards, after their long and hard experience in the transports, these soldiers had their arms clean and bright, and cartridge-boxes filled with forty rounds, while they aligned and dressed in line of battle as coolly and precisely as if on ordinary parade. Probably there was not a man among them who had not been 'in' a dozen times before. There was little fuss about it, and no noise of either bugling or verbal command. Then suddenly, at a 'right shoulder shift' and a 'double quick,' the line swept across the sandy plain which extended from the place of starting to the base of the huge mamelons which, running from sea to river, formed the northern side of the fort.

"Nearly all the guns upon the northern face had been dismounted or disabled by the severe bombardment; but when the assaulting line came near enough, the garrison opened on it with musketry, and a howitzer, which was run out from a sally-port, cut great gaps in the advancing line with grape and canister, leaving many a poor fellow behind with the salt sand drinking in his heart's blood.

"Such a charge soon carried them to the palisade at the foot of the great earthworks, and the pioneers' axes began to gleam in the western sun, as they chopped away at the palings, already shattered in some places by the bombardment. The fire of small arms now became incessant, as the assailants began to respond.

"After what seemed a long delay we saw the line pass through the obstruction, and, in another moment, they and their colors were seen on one of the western mamelons, sharply defined against the sky. Then there was a sharp musketry fight, and men, killed or wounded, rolled down the steep incline; yells of defiance and shouts of command grew louder and louder, and then there came a rush, a pell-mell struggle, and we saw the colors slowly rise, and then established on the top of the next mound. Then more fighting, another rush, and the next mound was taken, after the most determined resistance. Seeing this, General [Alfred H.] Terry signalled to fire into the easterly traverses and clear them out, which was done with wonderful precision, until the advancing fight rendered the shelling as dangerous to our own troops as to the enemy.

"The Confederates fought like tigers, and the sun went down and night closed in while this desperate infantry fight was going on, rendering it impossible to distinguish friends from foes by our glasses. Fearfully anxious, yet confident, we waited on the deck, listening to the varying sounds as the two parties fought at close quarters, guided in their fire by the flashes of their opponents' muskets. At last, about ten o'clock at night, there was tremendous cheering, and the tide of battle suddenly swept away down toward Federal Point, where the remnant of the garrison, about two thousand in number, laid down their arms. The surrender was instantly telegraphed by means of signal lanterns, and every ship sent up round after round of hearty cheers; not only for joy at the achievement, but because there was an end, at last, of the weary blockade, on that dangerous coast, of a most important point—so important, indeed, that Gen. Lee had telegraphed not long before, 'that it must be held at any cost, otherwise he must evacuate Richmond.' The Confederacy was by this capture completely isolated, and no more military supplies could go in, or cotton go out; and cotton meant gold, the sinews of war.

"In battery number four, as the painted board proclaimed it, was found a 150-pound Armstrong gun, which we were curious about, as we had exchanged compliments freely and frequently with it also. This piece bore the 'broad arrow'; showing it had passed the English government proof, and had Sir William Armstrong's name upon the trunnion. It was mounted on a splendid carriage, and was *said* to have been a gift from some English admirers to the Southern Confederacy. Armstrong guns, of less calibre than this, were found in several of the forts about Cape Fear. These forts were all taken or occupied after abandonment in a very few days after Fort Fisher fell."

144

In the picture, Mr. Davidson, the artist, shows the English Armstrong gun above mentioned, which was photographed as it stood in the traverse when captured. Charging from the beach are seen the marines as they attempt to break through the stockade and storm this portion of the fort.

THE COMPLETE COLOR PORTFOLIO OF

*"Prang's War Pictures"*

146

PLATE I.

*Sheridan's Final Charge at Winchester,* 1886. General Philip H. Sheridan loses his hat as he gallops forward to lead six thousand troops in the final, frenzied cavalry charge against Jubal Early's Confederate forces at the third Battle of Winchester, Virginia, on September 19, 1864. For this "most spirited picture," artist Thure de Thulstrup copied the brigade colors directly from the original flag on display at the West Point Museum and bathed the scene in what he called "atmospheric" autumn twilight. The officer on the white horse, sword held high, is Colonel Charles R. Lowell (nephew of the poet), and behind him is Brigadier General George Armstrong Custer. Note the Confederate defenders in the foreground, fallen, fleeing, or firing back near an abandoned caisson. Captain Theodore F. Rodenbough, who can be seen sitting erect on the brown horse to the right of Lowell, called this work "beautiful and truthful," commending its "exceptional degree of realism." Prang claimed that General John A. Logan "made the final corrections in the artist's sketch" of the scene. *(Library of Congress)*

PLATE 2.

*Battle of Fredericksburg* (also known as *Laying the Pontons* [sic] *at Fredericksburg)*, 1886. Confederate snipers on the shore below Fredericksburg, Virginia (visible in the distance), open fire at Union troops who can be seen massing in the foreground, preparing to ford the Rappahannock River on pontoon bridges. The chromo depicts the moment on December 11, 1862, when enemy sharpshooters kill one and wound several, including the detachment commander. The assault initially proved successful: Union forces occupied the town and captured thirty-one Confederates. Robert E. Lee was actually delighted that the Federals crossed the river to fight on his terms; another Confederate officer termed it a "great blunder." Sure enough, Union troops were soundly defeated, suffering more than twelve thousand casualties, at the battle that commenced on December 13. Union General Edward Ferrero, who was "on the spot" for the action portrayed, called the print "perfectly correct." *(Library of Congress)*

PLATE 3.

*Sheridan's Ride, October 19, 1864,* 1886. The *Text* to this picture did not much exaggerate when it claimed that Sheridan's fabled ride from Winchester to Cedar Creek had generally "escaped the notice of artist and author." Although the ride had rallied Union troops, inspiring a famous poem and several paintings, most printmakers had generally, inexplicably ignored the heroic incident until Prang adapted Thulstrup's watercolor for this chromo. This "dashing scene," Prang asserted, was designed to show the "*last quarter* on the home stretch of Sheridan's Ride," honoring "the wondrous power possessed and exercised at a critical moment by a born leader of men." Eyewitnesses recalled that soldiers "swung their caps around their heads and broke into cheers" as Sheridan dashed by astride his horse, Rienzi, and the print accurately portrayed their emotional response. But Sheridan waved his own hat that day, not the battle flag shown here, and he wore a beard, which the artist failed to represent. Nonetheless, a veteran of the incident testified that the picture "attained an exceptional degree of realism." *(Library of Congress)*

PLATE 4.

*Battle of Gettysburg, July 3, 1863*, 1887. The legendary fame of the Battle of Gettysburg was such that it is surprising that Prang did not portray it until the fourth in his series of war pictures. Appropriately, the chromo depicted the climactic action on the afternoon of the third day, showing Pickett's doomed charge, the so-called "high-water mark" of the Confederacy. Here, some eighteen thousand Confederates launch an all-out assault against Webb's Division (charging from left to right in the chromo), as Union General Winfield Scott Hancock (left foreground) arrives on the field to urge his defenders to resist. Cushing's battery has been all but destroyed, but the heroic "Philadelphia Brigade" holds the line until reenforcements can arrive to turn back the charge. "This picture . . . is of historic value," the *Text* proclaimed, adding that the print would prove "of great interest to all who were with, and who glory in, the achievements of the Army of the Potomac." As one veteran recalled, "individuality was drowned in a sea of clamor" that day, so the *Text* usefully included a two-page key (see page 71) to identify the officers, flags, and batteries portrayed in the chromo. (*Library of Congress*)

154

PLATE 5.

*Battle of Antietam*, 1887. Union troops advance fearlessly in the teeth of withering enemy fire around Dunker's Church at Sharpsburg, Maryland, on September 17, 1862, the bloodiest single day of fighting in the entire Civil War. The *Prospectus* to the Prang series identified the scene as representing the Union's final triumph after several attacks "around this now famous spot." Thus, the picture illustrated a bitter irony of the battle: that a great deal of it involved a place of peace, the small, white-washed German Baptist Brethren chapel, around which so much devastation exploded. Facing what one Confederate veteran recalled as an "artillery hell" on this spot, Hooker's forces reached as far as the abandoned Confederate caisson (top left) in the furious battle for the church and the surrounding woods. *(Library of Congress)*

156

PLATE 6.

*Battle of Spotsylvania and the Bloody Angle*, 1887. The American flag dominates this dramatic composition, which depicts Union troops, bayonets fixed, launching a surprise early-morning attack against a salient later named the "Bloody Angle," near Spotsylvania Court House, Virginia, on May 12, 1864, during the Wilderness Campaign. An eyewitness to the carnage later recalled that the Confederates defended their position with "the fury of a cyclone." The Prang *Prospectus* boasted that artist Thulstrup "invested his conception of this scene with a realism that conveys to the beholder a vivid impression of the desperate struggle. . . ." Indeed, few chromos in the Prang series illustrated such brutal hand-to-hand combat so realistically. Note, particularly, the gruesome depiction of the Union soldier stabbing a Confederate defender with his bayonet (left). *(Library of Congress)*

PLATE 7. (facing page)

*Battle of Chattanooga, November 25, 1863,* 1886. Generals George H. Thomas (right) and Gordon Granger (left) flank the diminutive General Ulysses S. Grant, wrapped in a light-blue coat, field glass lifted to his eyes, as the commanders survey the Union assault on Missionary Ridge. Writing in his memoirs, which appeared the year before this print was published, Grant recalled watching "eagerly to see the effect" of the Union effort to seize what another general called that "angry mountain." Note the exquisite attention to detail in this chromo: the orderly holding the three generals' horses in the foreground; the signal-flag officer (left) communicating to General Sherman in the distance below; the soldier (right) gripping the corps headquarters flag; and the puffs of smoke emanating almost picturesquely from enemy artillery on the mountain. Thomas's chief of staff called this a "beautiful lifelike picture," which ". . . conveys an excellent idea of the scene of that afternoon." *(Library of Congress)*

PLATE 8. (overleaf)

*Battle of Kenesaw Mountain,* 1887. From astride his noble black charger, the imposing General John A. Logan (left) orders the Federal XV Corps to charge the eastern end of Georgia's daunting Kenesaw Mountain (background, left) on June 27, 1864. Johnston's Confederates fire back with artillery shells, reminding the viewer of the considerable danger facing Union forces charging the summit that day. Note, too, the sobering sight of a casualty being carried to safety by two comrades in the left foreground. Prang's *Prospectus* claimed that Logan had "made the final corrections in the artist's sketch of this scene" a few months before his death. Appropriately, Thulstrup aptly called the original watercolor *Behind the Union Line,* for he often showed an affection for portraying small groups of high-ranking officers ordering troops to attack or defend their positions. The artist painted another version of the Battle of Kenesaw Mountain in 1889, depicting Sherman, not Logan, supervising the scene, but it was produced too late to be adapted for the Prang series. *(Library of Congress)*

PLATE 9. (overleaf facing page)

*Battle of Allatoona Pass,* or *Holding the Pass at Allatoona,* 1887. The desolated landscape of this vital railroad subdepot near Georgia's Kenesaw Mountain dominates Prang's scene of the Union repulse of a Confederate attack on October 5, 1864. Responding to General Sherman's plea, "Hold fast. We are coming," Brigadier General John M. Corse not only withstood the enemy bravely (inspiring a celebratory hymn, *Hold the Fort, For We Are Coming*), but launched the fierce counterattack depicted here, sending the Confederates reeling down the hill. To the right, the signal corps can be seen communicating with the main army. "The little redoubt," the Prang *Text* recalled, was soon "encumbered by the dead." But Sherman believed Corse's triumph demonstrated that fortified positions should be held "to the last" whenever possible. *(Library of Congress)*

158

PLATE 10.

*Battle of Atlanta*, or *Siege of Atlanta: An Artillery Review*, 1888. General William T. Sherman (center) listens to a report from an artillery officer as he calmly observes what he called "the slow and steady progress" of the bombardment of Atlanta in the late summer of 1864. Artist Thulstrup based the portrait on a wartime photograph but made the general look neater and less grizzled than he did in the original camera study, trimming his beard and straightening his collar. The other officers in the scene are (left to right) Brigadier General William F. Barry, chief of artillery; Brigadier General John M. Corse (the hero of Allatoona), inspector-general; Colonel L. M. Dayton, an aide-de-camp; and, next to Sherman, holding field glasses, Colonel Orlando M. Poe, his chief of engineers. Lieutenant Colonel Charles Ewing, another inspector-general and Sherman's brother-in-law, has his back to the viewer. "The portraits are given with careful detail," noted the *Prospectus*, "and the officers form a picturesque and historical group. . . ." *(Library of Congress)*

PLATE 11.

*Battle of Vicksburg*, or *Siege of Vicksburg: Assault on Fort Hill*, 1886. The Union tried a number of bold moves to capture "The Gibraltar of the West" before settling in for the long siege that finally culminated in its surrender in July, 1863. On June 25, Union General M. D. Leggett's Division used explosives to blow up the Confederate stronghold of Fort Hill. Then, battling volleys of hand grenades, he led his Illinois troops in a desperate attempt to storm the remaining, smoldering crater, the scene presented here. Starving Confederates bravely resisted with rifle fire and grenades, but Union soldiers ultimately prevailed after a bloody fight. Nine days later, Vicksburg finally surrendered to General Grant. This dramatic chromo, particularly the vignette showing the flag bearer reaching the apex of the crater, was brilliantly rendered. *(Library of Congress)*

166

PLATE 12.

*Battle of Shiloh. The Hornet's Nest*, 1888. The Union's stubborn, fearless defense of a thicket behind a sunken roadbed at Shiloh, Tennessee, on April 6, 1862, saved the day for Grant's beleaguered army, giving him time to regroup and win his first great victory. Bullets buzzed about these woods so noisily that survivors nicknamed the infamous place "The Hornet's Nest." Thulstrup's "spirited picture" depicted Captain Andrew Hickenlooper (left center, sword in hand), ordering an artilleryman to fetch additional ammunition. Astride the horse at right is General Benjamin M. Prentiss, who had been ordered by Grant to hold the position for as long as possible. Prentiss ultimately surrendered the remains of his force of Iowa troops, but not before his tenacity held off, and ultimately prevented, Confederate victory. "From this position," recalled a survivor, "blazed for six hours sheets of flame . . . a murderous storm of shot and shell, and musketry fire, which no living thing could quell." *(Library of Congress)*

168

PLATE 13.

*Capture of New Orleans. Farragut Passing the Forts by Night. April 24, 1862, 1886.* As "white smoke rolled and heaved in vast volumes along the shuddering waters," according to one eyewitness, Admiral David Glasgow Farragut's flagship *Hartford* steams past Forts Jackson and St. Philip on the Mississippi River. Farragut's vessel comes under furious attack from the ironclad *Louisiana* (left), while the ram *Manassas* (right) races into the fray. This bravura print shows the moment when Farragut's vessel, run aground under a barrage of shelling from the forts, comes under further attack from a dangerous fire raft, pushed against her hull and setting her afire. Finally, the *Hartford* eases free, sinks the *Mosher* (left foreground), the tugboat that had nudged the fire barge against her side, and slips downriver toward the crucial conquest of New Orleans. Julian O. Davidson's "brilliant representation," on which the chromo was based, took pains to show how the violent gunfire lit up the sky, turning night into day. *(The Lincoln Museum, Fort Wayne, Indiana)*

PLATE 14.

*Battle Between the "Monitor" and "Merrimac," March 8, 1862*, or *"The Monitor and Merrimac." The First Fight Between Ironclads,* 1886. The Confederate ironclad *Virginia*, or as it is more often remembered, the *Merrimac*, exchanges fire at close range with the Union ironclad *Monitor*, at the dramatic Battle of Hampton Roads, Virginia. Although the warships dueled to a draw that day, the encounter was celebrated as an epochal milestone: the first fight between iron ships at sea. Note that the hulking *Merrimac* belches ugly black smoke, while the sleek *Monitor* spews symbolically pure white smoke, a reminder of the print's Union perspective. J. O. Davidson, who painted the original watercolor on which the chromo was modeled, meant the work to portray the action "near the close of the fight, when the Monitor, ranging alongside the Merrimac, is firing at short range." Davidson based his work on interviews with the *Monitor*'s surviving crewmembers, as well as recollections by its inventor, John Ericsson, and one of the *Merrimac*'s builders, John L. Porter. Davidson also acknowledged a debt to marine artist Francis A. Silva, who had observed and sketched the actual battle from the shoreline at nearby Newport News. *(Library of Congress)*

172

PLATE 15.

*Battle of Mobile Bay. August 5, 1864*, 1886. The mighty Union naval squadron under Farragut's command exchanges hellish fire with Fort Morgan (left) at one of the most dramatic naval battles of the Civil War. The warship *Brooklyn* (right) leads the awesome line of Union warships, followed closely by Farragut's flagship, the *Hartford*. A mine has already claimed the Union ironclad *Tecumseh*, shown careening near the center of the scene, but Farragut has famously responded, "Damn the torpedoes! Full speed ahead!" The danger is intensified by the sight of the Confederate ironclad *Tennessee*, arriving on the scene to join the fray, typically emitting ominous black smoke. Another virtuoso scene by J. O. Davidson, this chromo presents the mighty Confederate fortification as a foe worthy of the brave Union admiral and his armada. The battle claimed more than three hundred Federal casualties but ranked as a strategic and moral victory for the Union. *(Library of Congress)*

PLATE 16.

*Kearsarge and Alabama*, 1887. Although the duel between the Union sloop and the Confederate "pirate ship" took place in the English Channel off the coast of distant Cherbourg, France, the triumph of the *Kearsarge* on June 19, 1864, thrilled the North and undoubtedly helped the pro-war Republican Party win the elections that fall. The engagement inspired many artists, who typically showed the two vessels locked in mortal combat. J. O. Davidson innovatively chose to portray instead the moment when "the scourge of American commerce" lurches, bow upward, before sinking to the bottom. Moreover, Davidson painted the scene from the unique perspective of the crew of the victorious *Kearsarge*. On its bloodstained deck, a gun-loader can be seen waving his cap triumphantly. Although the picture was derivative (Davidson copied an old *Harper's Weekly* woodcut of the foundering commerce raider), the artist vivified his version with telling details, like the pile of canister visible in the foreground and the highly individualized portraits of crewmen laboring on guns and lines or aiding wounded comrades. Commander John A. Winslow can be seen at left; nearby is an African American sailor. The *Kearsarge* boasted an integrated crew, and Prang was not averse to illustrating this point. *(The Lincoln Museum, Fort Wayne, Indiana)*

176

PLATE 17.

*Battle of Port Hudson. Passing the River Batteries,* 1887. "It seemed as if the whole heavens were ablaze with thunder and lightning," a Confederate veteran recalled of the night of March 14, 1863, when Admiral Farragut's fleet ran the gauntlet past a formidable Louisiana fort guarding the Mississippi River. Farragut ordered his precious gunboats lashed to the side of his larger vessels to shield them from the withering enemy mortar fire, a detail J. O. Davidson barely conveys in a scene intended to show the flagship *Hartford* reaching safety. Instead, the artist daringly shows the fighting from the Confederate point of view, portraying a swarm of soldiers loading and firing their deadly accurate batteries and one (lower right) recoiling from a blast of return gunfire. The Union fleet suffered heavy casualties that day but, in surviving the onslaught and moving upriver, could legitimately claim success. *(Library of Congress)*

178

PLATE 18.

*Capture of Fort Fisher,* 1887. This depiction of the Union naval and marine assault on this North Carolina Confederate coastline stronghold on January 15, 1865, gave artist Davidson his one opportunity to demonstrate prowess at depicting war on land as well as at sea. Rising to the occasion, he barely suggested the presence (background) of the Union's large North Atlantic Squadron. Instead, he focused on sailors and marines (right) bursting through the wooden palisades defending the northeastern salient of Fort Fisher, enduring ravaging fire from Confederate infantry perched on the traverse, and coming face-to-face with a 150-pound English Armstrong gun aimed directly at the beach. The Confederates actually repulsed this oceanside assault but succumbed to a later attack from the opposite, river side of the peninsula. The capture of Fort Fisher effectively ended blockade running, choked off the flow of supplies to the South, and hastened the fall of the Confederacy, making this a fitting scene with which to end the Prang series. *(Library of Congress)*

# INDEX